From the libra

D1122279

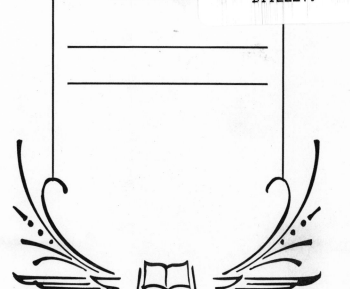

THE
REVEALING
WORD

The REVEALING WORD

A Dictionary of Metaphysical Terms

Charles Fillmore Reference Library

UNITY® Books

Unity Village, Missouri

The Revealing Word: A Dictionary of Metaphysical Terms is a member of the Charles Fillmore Reference Library.

Charles Fillmore was an innovative thinker, a pioneer in metaphysical thought at a time when most religious thought in America was entirely orthodox. He was a lifelong advocate of the open, inquiring mind, and he took pride in keeping abreast of the latest scientific and educational discoveries and theories. Many years ago he wrote, "What you think today may not be the measure for your thought tomorrow"; and it seems likely that were he to compile this book today, he might use different metaphors, different scientific references, and so on. *7/98*

Truth is changeless. Those who knew Charles Fillmore best believe that he would like to be able to rephrase some of his observations for today's readers, thus giving them the added effectiveness of contemporary thought. But the ideas themselves—the core of Charles Fillmore's writings—are as timeless now (and will be tomorrow) as when they were first published.

First printing 1959; thirteenth printing 1997

ISBN 0-87159-006-9
Canada GST R132529033

Unity Books feels a sacred trust to be a healing presence in the world. By printing with biodegradable soybean ink on recycled paper, we believe we are doing our part to be wise stewards of our Earth's resources.

FOREWORD

The Revealing Word offers Truth students the metaphysical meanings and uses of words and phrases that frequently appear in Unity publications, and many that appear in the Bible. Whereas Unity's *Metaphysical Bible Dictionary* explains the esoteric meanings of scriptural proper names, *The Revealing Word* is devoted mostly to common names. In addition to words that have religious significance, hundreds of words that are in everyday use appear in this book. Thus the reader is given inner meanings that he or she can apply to daily living. All things in life are expressed in words. Equipped with the inner meanings of words, a person can control all the issues of his or her life, from the insignificant to the great. (Bible quotations in this book are from the American Standard Version.)

A

abate—To lessen; to moderate. In making a demonstration, when we reach the point where the mind changes from the negative to the positive state the troubled thoughts begin to abate. A certain set of negative ideas has run its course, and the restorative thought forces are in evidence.

Abba—A word of endearment signifying father. It is only as we come to know our sonship, our true relation to God, that we enter into the consciousness of love and tender affiliation with Spirit, signified by the word *Abba.* (see Mark 14:36)

abdicate—To let go; to relinquish; to renounce. The ability to abdicate is twofold in action: it eliminates the error, and it expands the good. When the ego consciously lets go and willingly gives up its personal ideas and loves, it has fulfilled the law of denial and is restored to the Father's house.

abide—To continue in a fixed thought of God, the All-Good; to dwell in the Christ consciousness. "If ye abide in me, and my words abide in you, ask whatsoever ye will, and it shall be done unto you" (John 15:7).

abiding—A conscious centering of the mind in divine Principle within us by means of repeated affirmations of our faith and trust in Principle.

abiding Presence—Christ, the presence of light, peace, joy, love, life, and substance that is ever within, about, before, and beside man. (see *presence of God*)

Absolute, the—Divine Mind; unlimited Principle; the almighty One; the all-pervading Spirit; the Infinite; the Eternal; the Supreme Being. The one ultimate creative Mind; the Source of all things. That which is unconditioned, unlimited, unrestricted, and free from all limitations. The self-existent God.

Absolute, to place judgment in the—The metaphysician finds it necessary to place his judgment in the Absolute in order to demonstrate His supreme power. This is accomplished by first declaring that one's judgment is spiritual and not material, that its origin is in God, that all its conclusions are based on Truth, and that they are absolutely free from prejudice, false sympathy, or personal ignorance.

Absolute, treating in the—Treating in the consciousness of the Spirit of God; affirming the absolute Truth of Being for man.

Absolute, unification of man with the—Man unifies himself with the Absolute through recognition that he is the son and heir of the Father, in whose image and likeness he was created. By realizing the Mind of Christ, he becomes one with the Absolute.

abstract, the—The realm of pure ideas such as goodness, purity, wisdom, and love.

abundance, spiritual—Ideas in consciousness of the omnipresent supply and support of the one Mind; invisible substance, with infinite capacity of expansion when held in mind, affirmed, and praised. "All things whatsoever the Father hath are mine" (John 16:15).

abundance, steps in demonstrating—First, we must recognize abundance as an idea that is real and has the power to expand. Then, we must talk abundance—choose words representing abundance—and thus build up an invisible world of substance. In this way, we build or form in our mind that which draws to us an abundance of every good thing. "For whosoever hath, to him shall be given" (Luke 8:18).

accident—An unfortunate event that takes place without our conscious foreknowledge.

accidents, cause and cure of—The cause of all accidents lies in sense consciousness. To be free from all accidents, we must raise our consciousness, so that it is spiritually positive and Christlike. Then we shall attract only good.

accuser—Opposer; hater; an enemy. (see *Devil* and *Satan*) The accuser is overcome by casting him down in the name of Jesus Christ.

achievement, universal desire for—The craving for accomplishment, innate in every man. The universal desire for worth-while achievement, giving a mighty impulse to all things, is divinely good.

acquisitiveness—The desire to acquire. It is a legitimate faculty of mind, but covetousness is the Judas trait. When a man seeks to acquire from God only, acquisitiveness builds up his consciousness, but when he oversteps the law and seeks that which belongs to another his acquisitiveness becomes a destroyer. (see *covetousness*)

activity, spiritual—Thoughts in relation to spiritual Principle. Mind movement in accordance with the activity of Divine Mind.

Adam—Red; reddish. The first movement of mind in its contact with life and substance. Adam was created from the "dust of the ground" (Gen. 2:7). Dust represents the radiant earth or substance. When spiritual man (I AM) enters into this substance and makes use of the God ideas inherent in him, he brings forth the ideal body in its elemental perfection. Adam was first perfect as an idea in elemental divinity.

Adam man—Unregenerate sense man; antichrist: the man who has fallen away from spirituality. Originally Adam was the spiritually illumined man of God. The Adam man was primitively identified with an infinite capacity for expansion. When he recognizes his identity as spiritual he expands in divine order and brings forth only good.

Adam man, ills of—The many ills of the Adam man grew out of his belief that he could satisfy and nourish himself with material food and drink alone. To feed the body is not enough. The spiritual man hungers for the bread of life and thirsts for living water, even the Word of God.

Adam man, transformation of—We are not to erase Adam, but we are to transform him by the renewing of our mind. "And be not fashioned according to this world: but be ye transformed by the renewing of your mind, that ye may prove what is the good and acceptable and perfect will of God" (Rom. 12:2).

adjustment—The rearrangement of thoughts according to the divine order of the Christ Mind; a bringing of man's consciousness into exact correspondence with God's perfect harmony, or heaven. "And the crooked shall become straight, and the rough ways smooth" (Luke 3:5).

adultery—Mixed thoughts, errors that have their existence in the unregenerated feelings; thoughts that have not come under the dominion of the I AM.

Adversary, the—The vain imagination that there could, in reality, be anything opposed to Divine Mind, or could be any separation of man from it, led to the forming of a state of mind that is described in the Bible as the "adversary." We find that the various names—*Satan; Devil; Adversary; accuser; carnal mind; old man; man of sin; and personality*—all refer to the consciousness that man has built up in his ignorance of his true estate.

affirm—To hold steadfast in mind or to speak aloud a statement of Truth.

affirm the salvation of the Lord—To realize silently and to declare audibly that the Christ within us is taking charge of all our affairs.

affirmation—A positive statement of Truth. By the use of affirmations we claim and appropriate that which is ours in Truth. (see *denial*)

affirmation, act of—The "yes" action of the mind; the act of affirming; the declaring of Truth; the mental movement that asserts confidently and persistently the

Truth of Being in the face of all appearances to the contrary.

affirmation and denial—Two movements of the mind that express power to accept or to reject, to lay hold of or to let go. (see *denial*)

affirmation, how made—Affirmations do not have to be made only in set terms such as, *"I affirm my body to be spiritual."* The sum total of thought in all its positive aspects composes the affirmations that bring ideas into form.

affirmation, purpose of—To establish in consciousness a broad understanding of the divine principles on which all life and existence depend. By affirming Truth we are lifted out of false thinking into the consciousness of Spirit.

affirmation, remedial effects of—All unrighteous conditions may be adjusted through affirming the power of the great universal Spirit of justice. Affirm: *"The infinite Spirit of love and justice is now operating in all my affairs. and all is well."*

age—A cycle or a dispensation. Jesus was acquainted with cycles or ages of spiritual development of which the natural man knew nothing. Jesus came at the end of an age. Age to mortal man is the measurement of the life or existence of a person or thing. It is based on the false concept of time as reality. "What is the signal of Your presence, and the completion of this age?" (Matt. 24:3, Fenton.)

air—The deific breath of God. It symbolizes a purifying, vitalizing power that revives and makes alive.

alchemy, divine—Transmutation; changing in action and in character from the mortal into the spiritual. It has been said that the mind is the crucible in which the ideal is transmuted into the real.

alcoholism—A diseased condition brought about by one who, thirsting for the true stimulation of Spirit, resorts to the excessive use of false stimulants, such as alcoholic beverages. The way to demonstrate over this condition is to turn wholeheartedly to Spirit and to realize and to affirm that the desire for false stimulants is dissolved and dissipated and that the pure spiritual life of Christ satisfies and uplifts.

allegiance to the Father—The consciousness that divine wisdom is guiding the universe and man, which gives man a feeling of security. Allegiance to the Father signifies a constant devotion to and trust in the Father.

allegory—A symbolical representation of Truth. "Which things contain an allegory" (Gal. 4:24).

All-Good—Divine Mind; God; the principle of divine benevolence that permeates the universe.

almighty—All-powerful; having all power or force to accomplish anything. All things are possible with God, because He is infinitely all-mighty. All the power, all the force, all the might of the universe are God's; He is, in truth, almighty God. "Jehovah appeared to Abram, and said unto him, I am God Almighty" (Gen. 17:1).

Alpha and Omega—The beginning and the end; the Son of God; all in all. "I am the Alpha and the Omega" (Rev. 22:13).

altar—Stabilized place of worship. A fixed, definite center in consciousness; the place in consciousness where we meet the Lord and are willing to give up our sins, to give up the lower for the higher, the personal for the impersonal.

The altar mentioned in Rev. 11:1 symbolizes the consciousness of full consecration that takes place first in the temple of worship within: "Present your bodies a living sacrifice, holy, acceptable to God, *which is* your spiritual service" (Rom. 12:1).

altar, brazen, of temple worship—Represents the generative life.

altar, golden, of incense—Symbolizes the establishing of permanent resolutions of purity and covenants with the higher law of obedience, although it may entail daily sacrifice. (This applies to the altar of the burnt offerings also.)

altar, to an unknown God—A yearning to know the unrevealed Spirit and a reaching out for a fuller realization of its source.

alternate between good and evil—To swing the mind from good to evil and vice versa, with consequent variation in the application of Truth principles. Alternation is fatal to realization. "For let not that man think that he shall receive anything of the Lord; a double-minded man, unstable in all his ways" (James 1:7, 8).

ambition—A subtle mental force that drives men toward their goals. If it is dedicated wholly to Spirit and acts from Principle, it will work for good. If its motto is, "The end justifies the means," it is a menace.

ancestors—Forefathers. Those who think of themselves as descended from human ancestors are in bondage to all the limitations of those ancestors, regardless of their claims to the contrary. It is a falling short of the full stature of man to regard himself as descending from the human family. This is the sin that keeps the majority of men in bondage to sense consciousness.

angel—A messenger of God; the projection into consciousness of a spiritual idea direct from the Fountainhead, Jehovah. "And there appeared unto him an angel of the Lord standing on the right side of the altar" (Luke 1:11). The word of Truth, in which is centered the power of God to overcome all limited beliefs and conditions.

angel, of Jehovah—The quickening thought of God appearing in the form of light or divine intelligence, intuition, and understanding.

angels, ascending and descending—The imaging power of the mind receiving divine ideas and reflecting them into the consciousness.

angels, office of—To guard, to direct, and to redeem the natural forces of the body and mind, which have in them the future of the whole man.

anointed of God, the—One who is conscious of the real spiritual outpouring from the source of his being; a consecrated person, "The Spirit of the Lord is upon me, because he anointed me" (Luke 4:18).

anointing—A symbolical expression of the pouring out of the spirit of love on one who has faith in God. Rubbing with oil; consecrating the body with the living Spirit of Christ. "But thou, when thou fastest, anoint thy head, and wash thy face" (Matt. 6:17).

antichrist—That which denies or opposes the idea that the Christ dwells in and is the true self of each individual. The active effort in the world to exalt death and to delude men into believing that death is the way to eternal life is an instance of work that is antichrist. Such a thought is opposed to Christ. Jesus came to deliver the human race from death and to fulfill in man God's perfect will, abundant life. The antichrist thoughts must be persistently denied. The perfect will of God for all men is abundant life, not death.

anxiety—A form of fear; a negative mental attitude that keeps God's good from man.

apostles—Those sent forth; messengers; ambassadors; active spiritual thoughts. Jesus conferred this title on the Twelve whom He sent forth to teach and to heal.

In order to command our powers and to bring them into unity of action, we must know what they are and their respective places on the staff of Being. The Grand Man, Christ, has twelve powers of fundamental ideas, represented in the history of Jesus by the Twelve Apostles. So each of us has twelve faculties or fundamental ideas to make manifest, to bring out, and to use in the attainment of his ideals. There are innumerable other ideas, but each one stems from some one of these fundamental ideas.

Jesus' twelve apostles were: Peter (faith); Andrew (strength); James, son of Zebedee (wisdom or judgment); John (love); Philip (power); Bartholomew (imagination); Thomas (understanding); Matthew (will); James (order); Simon the Cananaean (zeal); Thaddaeus (renunciation or elimination); and Judas (life conserver). (see *disciple, calling of*)

appetite—Either the craving of the sense man for fulfillment of his fleshly desires or the hunger and thirst of the spirit for its divine inheritance. "But he awaketh . . . and, behold, he is faint, and his soul hath appetite" (Isa. 29:8).

appetite, carnal or sensual—A hunger and thirst for sensual pleasures; misdirected effort to obtain satisfaction through feeding the insatiable sense man. All indulgence of such appetite must be denied out of man's consciousness before Christ can be manifested.

appreciation—The act of appreciating; esteeming. Spiritually, man's mind esteems to a great measure the loveliness and power of omnipresent God, All-Good. "I will give thee thanks with my whole heart" (Psalms 138:1).

appropriation—The act of taking possession of something. To appropriate the word of Truth is to take the substance of the word into one's mind and heart.

ark—A holy place; a sanctuary; a tabernacle; the Christ center within wherein man is one with pure Being.

ark, Noah's—Symbolizes the spiritual part of oneself, built in the midst of the flood of error. One builds one's ark on the scientific understanding of the wisdom, presence, and power of God and on the affirmations of what one is in Spirit.

The only refuge from the Flood (see Gen. 6:18) was the ark of Jehovah. The ark represents a positive, saving state of consciousness, which agrees with or forms a covenant with the principle of Being, with subconscious inspiration, with Christ. This ark is the product of "rest" (Noah) in the spiritual part of us, right in the midst of the flood of error.

Ark of the Covenant—Represents the original spark of divinity in man's being, which is a sacred and holy thing. On its development depends man's immortality. The original spark (Ark of the Covenant) occupies the most holy place in the body temple and must be cared for with great devotion; otherwise, the spiritual forces are scattered.

No human hand is allowed to touch this ark of the covenant. No human thought can enter the sacred precincts, which are kept veiled from all eyes.

armor of God—The robe of righteousness. Error cannot enter the consciousness that is strongly fortified with the light, life, power, and substance of Spirit.

ascension—The ascending or progressive unfoldment of man from the animal to the spiritual. It is measured by three degrees or states of consciousness: first, the animal; second, the mental or psychical; and third, the spiritual. Jesus first manifested Himself as the man on the physical plane, from which He was resurrected to the mental or psychical; from thence He ascended to the spiritual.

asceticism—The practice of severe self-denial; the attempt to deny the body itself as an evil thing instead of beholding it as the sacred temple of the living God to be revered, respected, and loved.

aspirations—The deep longing of man for union with his source, with his Father-Mother, God.

"As the hart panteth after the water brooks,
So panteth my soul after thee, O God.
My soul thirsteth for God, for the living God"
(Psalms 42:1, 2).

ass—In Oriental countries in Bible times kings and rulers rode the ass, and it was the accepted bearer of royalty. The animal part of the human consciousness is typified by the ass, and the purpose of Jesus' riding an ass into Jerusalem was to portray the mastery by the I AM of the animal nature and its manifestation (colt). Jerusalem is the city of peace or spiritual consciousness. The characteristics of the ass are stubbornness, persistency, and endurance. To ride these is to make them obedient to one's will.

association, spiritual—Living in an uninterrupted relationship with ideas that come into consciousness from God.

astrology—"The pseudo science which treats of the influence of the stars upon human affairs, and of foretelling terrestrial events by their position and aspects" (Webster). Astrology represents the belief in man that his good depends wholly on something outside himself— his ruling star, fate, providence—instead of depending on the power of his own thoughts to establish within himself and his world what he wills.

It is true that we are in sympathy with all nature, which includes the earth, the sun, the moon, and the stars. These are all ensouled, and their actions can affect us when we do not believe in a higher power. But there is a higher power in everyone: Spirit. In Genesis it is stated that spiritual man, the image-and-likeness man, was given dominion over all creation.

astronomy—"The science which treats of the celestial bodies, their magnitudes, motions, constitution, etcetera" (Webster).

The material universe is only the outpicturing of the spiritual universe. The pulsations of the spiritual forces impinge on and sway men, nations, and planets according to laws whose sweep in space and time is so stupendous as to be beyond the ken or comprehension of astronomy. But the fact should not be overlooked that higher astronomy had its votaries in the past. The Magi and the illumined sages of Chaldea and Egypt had astronomical knowledge of universal scope.

There is evidence that proves that the sages of the distant past knew a higher astronomy than do we of this age and that they predicted the future of this planet through cycles and aeons—its nights of mental darkness and the dawn of its spiritual day—with the same accuracy that our astronomers do its present-day planetary revolutions.

Jesus evidently understood this higher astronomy, and He knew that His work as a teacher and demonstrator of spiritual law was related to it, yet not controlled by it. He co-operated with the "law . . . and the prophets," as far as they went, but He knew the higher law of the Christ man and affirmed His supremacy in the words, "All authority hath been given unto me in heaven and on earth" (Matt. 28:18).

atmosphere—Individually, an extension of consciousness; collectively, the pervading influence of the predominating thoughts.

atom—"One of the small parts out of which any physical quantity is built up" (Webster). A particle charged with tremendous energy that may be released and made to give to man powers beyond expression. Jesus used the dynamic power of thought to break the bonds of the atoms composing the few loaves and fishes of the boy's lunch—and five thousand persons were fed. Material science says that each atom of matter has force and intelligence and a certain individuality; hence, it is a form of mind.

atonement—Reconciliation between God and man through Christ; the uniting of our consciousness with the higher consciousness. Jesus became the way by which all who accept Him may "pass over" to the higher consciousness. We have atonement through Him.

attainment, intellectual—Intellectual attainments are

not in themselves of use in matters spiritual. They have their end in teaching the student how to command his faculties and to bring them into subjection. We must drop them out of our mind as quickly as we can and be willing to commence anew in the school of the higher life. Let us affirm often: "I am meek and lowly of heart. *I am led of the Spirit.*"

attainment, spiritual—A laying hold of the high and lofty ideas of the Christ Mind; the bringing of spiritual ideas into manifestation in one's mind, body, and affairs.

attention—(see *concentration*)

attitude—The state of mind in relation to some matter or situation; a mental position. Attitude of mind toward environment determines the nature of man's environment. A positive attitude draws the good; a negative attitude brings its train of sin, sickness, poverty, and death. "For as he thinketh within himself, so is he" (Prov. 23:7).

attributes of Being—That which is inherent in the twelve powers of faculties.

augury—The blind following of the commands of some omen or voice, not of Spirit.

aura—The thought emanation that surrounds every person. As to whether it is an illumined aura, or medium, or dark and cloudy depends on the dominant thought force of each person. The aura around the bodies of sincere, honest persons is usually bright blue or some modification of blue. The aura is not visible to all persons, but only to those who have their psychical nature quickened on the spiritual plane.

There are in the world today men and women who have followed the teaching of Jesus and developed in their bodies a superenergy or life that not only permeates the physical structure but envelops it in a luminous aura that can be and is felt by both themselves and others. Spirit reveals that spiritual thinking breaks open the physical cells and atoms and releases their imprisoned life, which originally came from Divine Mind. Jesus carried this process so far that His whole body was transformed and became a conscious part of the Father's life and intelligence. (see *halo*)

aura, how created—Prayer liberates the energies pent up in the mind and body. Those who pray much create a spiritual aura that eventually envelops the whole body. The bands of light painted by artists around the heads of saints are not imaginary; they actually exist and are visible to the sharp eye of the painter. Luke testifies (9:29) that when Jesus was praying "his countenance was altered, and his raiment *became* white *and* dazzling." After Moses had been praying on the mountain his face shone so brightly that the people could not look at it, and he had to wear a veil.

authority—Rightful power; mastery; or dominion. "For he taught them as having authority" (Mark 1:22).

authority, having—Inspired by Spirit within. The Spirit of truth is the one and only authority in the study of Truth. (see John 16:13)

authority, parental—Human parental authority is a thought of bondage or slavery in mortal consciousness based on desire of parents to domineer and to wield power. Divine parental authority is child guidance based on love and understanding. It includes willingness to grant freedom to the child by helping him to know and to live Truth.

autosuggestion—The conscious impression of selected thoughts on the subconscious mind by oneself.

avarice—Inordinate greed for material riches. (Symbolized by "the money-changers.") The avaricious suffer most in body and are the most difficult to heal, because of the mental bias that prompts them to get all things as cheaply as possible, including the kingdom of heaven.

avarice, how to be free from—Establish in consciousness the idea of giving generously and freely, not from compulsion or for the sake of reward but from the pure love of giving.

awakening, spiritual—Becoming conscious of the things of Spirit, or God.

B

Baal worship—Putting nature before God in earth, air, and water; giving the substance of mind and body to the things of sense. It is a form of idolatry. "Thou shalt have no other gods before me" (Exod. 20:3).

babe—Metaphysically, a new state of consciousness; innocent and childlike.

babe in Christ—One whose face is turned toward the light, but who has not yet come into a deep understanding of Truth.

baptism—The spiritual cleansing of the mind. Typifies the cleansing power and work of Spirit that redeems men from sin. It is the first step in the realization of Truth. When the baptizing power of the word is poured on a center in consciousness, it dissolves all material thought, and through this cleansing, purifying process, the individual is prepared to see and to discern spiritually.

The two baptisms, those of John and Jesus, represent the two common steps in spiritual development, denial and affirmation, or the dropping of the old and laying hold of the new. In the first baptism, that of John, through the power of the word, the sense man is erased from consciousness, and the mind is purged and made ready for the second baptism, that of Jesus. In the second baptism, the creative law of divine affirmation, set into action by supreme Mind, lights its fires at the center of man's being, and when thus kindled raises soul and body to a high degree of purity. This process is known as regeneration.

baptism, Pentecostal—The great initial outpouring of

Spirit that took place more than nineteen centuries ago. The primal baptism of the Holy Spirit. (see Acts 2:1-4)

baptism, the Holy Spirit—A quickening of the spiritual nature that is reflected in mind and body. Spiritual baptism has power; it is affirmative; it is positive. This outpouring of the Holy Spirit is the second baptism. Christ represents this phase of baptism. It is the most precious gift of God and comes to those who steadfastly seek first the kingdom of God and His righteousness. "He shall baptize you in the Holy Spirit" (Matt. 3:11).

beatitudes, Jesus'—Jesus in exaltation is blessing spiritual man with the attributes of God and also blessing the natural man with the attributes of the spiritual man. (see Matt. 5:3-11)

beauty, spiritual—The loveliness of God beheld in His creations by the eye of man. Spiritual man beholds this divine loveliness everywhere. "He hath made everything beautiful in its time" (Eccles. 3:11).

beholding—We are transformed by beholding. Whatever we persistently behold we manifest. Our looking into the perfect pattern, the indwelling Christ, and beholding His perfection transforms us into His likeness.

Being—God; the Mind of the universe composed of archetype ideas: life, love, wisdom, substance, Truth, power, peace, and so forth. Being is omnipresent, omnipotent, omniscient; it is the fullness of God, the All-Good.

Being, personal and impersonal nature of—Being is not only impersonal Principle as far as its inherent and undeviating laws are concerned, but also personal as far as its relation to each of us is concerned. We as individuals do actually become a focus of universal Spirit.

Being, the law of growth and—Being exists under two phases: invisible and visible, abstract and concrete. The visible comes forth from the invisible, and this coming forth is always according to a universal method of growth from minute generative centers. From center to circumference is the plan of procedure throughout the universe. To study form alone and to expect to learn from it and its evolutions the secret of existence does not enable one to catch sight of Spirit moving upon every generating center.

belief—An inner acceptance of an idea as true. Belief is closely related to faith. Belief functions both consciously and subconsciously. Many false individual and race beliefs are very active below the conscious level. To erase these hidden error beliefs, a comprehensive program of denial is necessary.

belief in separateness, results of—The belief in separateness from God Mind leads to ignorance and death. All intelligence and life are derived from the one Mind. When man thinks of himself as being alone, he cuts himself off in consciousness from the fount of inspiration. "For apart from me ye can do nothing" (John 15:5).

believe on the Son—We must come to His terms of expression. We do not believe that there are other sons wiser than He and that from them we can get wisdom, guidance, and understanding. We believe that He is, as far as we are concerned, the only begotten Son of the Father.

Bethesda, Pool of—"House of mercy; house of healing." Represents the realization in consciousness that our life is being constantly purified, healed, and made new by the activity of mind. Physically, this is expressed in the purification and upbuilding of the blood by its coming in contact with the oxygen of the air in the lungs.

Bible—The sacred and inspired Scriptures of the Christian religion. It is a divine "book of life" rather than merely a history of people, and it bears "witness unto the word" of God (Acts 14:3).

Bible characters—The characters of the Bible represent ideas in one's own mind. When this symbolism is understood one can follow the characters in their various movements and thus find the way to solve all one's life's problems.

Bible, place in Truth study—The Bible is a recital of what has taken place in the consciousness of man, of the results of his working, either intelligently with the law or unintelligently against it, in seeking his own salvation. It gives an explanation of spiritual law as applied to man and tells him how to find the kingdom of heaven within.

Bible, spiritual interpretation of the—A spiritual interpretation of the Bible demands that the meaning of every figure, type, parable, and symbol must be in harmony with the fundamental principles of Being.

birth, new—The awakening of man to a consciousness of his unity with the one universal Spirit; the change from mortal to spiritual consciousness through the begetting and quickening power of the word of Truth. It is the change that comes here and now. Jesus made no mention of resurrection after death as having any part in the new birth. "Except one be born anew, he cannot see the kingdom of God" (John 3:3).

birth, new, change following—When man is begotten and born of the Word he is no longer "flesh . . . as grass" (I Pet. 1:24) but is eternal and abiding, not subject to death and corruption.

birth, new, effect of—Begetting and quickening take place in man's inner consciousness, but the process of being "born anew" (John 3:3) includes the whole man, spirit, soul, and body. To be born again is to be made "a new creature" (II Cor. 5:17) having "this mind in you, which was also in Christ Jesus" (Phil. 2:5) and a body like unto His glorious body.

black magic—Jesus said that the kingdom of heaven had been taken by violence and force. "And from the days of John the Baptist until now the kingdom of heaven suffereth violence, and men of violence take it by force" (Matt. 11:12). It is possible to use the life, sub- stance, and power that form the basis of the kingdom of heaven in selfish ways. This is black magic and is the work of the selfish personality that Jesus refers to in Matt. 10:28, "Fear him who is able to destroy both soul and body in hell."

blasphemy—Impious or irreverent thoughts toward God, such as sickness, poverty, death. "But the blasphemy against the Spirit shall not be forgiven" (Matt. 12:31).

bless—To invoke good upon; to call forth the action of God; to confer God's good on something or someone.

blessedness of God—The joy that comes from God to those whose thoughts are stayed on Him. "Everlasting joy shall be unto them" (Isa. 61:7).

blessing, power of—Blessing imparts the quickening spiritual power that produces growth and increase. It is the power of multiplication.

blood—Expresses a spiritual principle that has been introduced into the race mind through the purified Jesus. It is a spiritual principle in that it rests on pure ideals; yet it is manifested in mind and body in concrete form when rightly appropriated. That it can be appropriated and used to the purification of the mind and the healing of the body, thousands are proving in this day.

Through His experience on the Cross, where His pre- cious blood was spilled, through His suffering there, Jesus lowered His consciousness to the consciousness of the race, thereby administering to the whole race a blood transfusion, imparting to man the properties of Being that will restore him to his divine estate. Such a transfusion not only revives us in temporal ills, but begins in the body a purifying and energizing process that will finally save us from death.

blood of Christ—The life contained in God's Word. Therefore, it is spiritual energy that purifies and redeems man by pouring into his life currents a new and purer stream. This divine energy cleanses the consciousness of dead works to enable man to serve the living God.

blood of Jesus—That which represents the principle of eternal life. Jesus raised the life activity of His blood and revealed its spiritual potency. In this respect it became part of the spiritual life of the race and is thus accessible to all persons. It is after this manner that we drink His blood. "Except ye eat the flesh of the Son of man and drink his blood, ye have not life in yourselves" (John 6:53).

blood of the Lamb—The innocent, undefiled life, or the primal life of Being, which Jesus made accessible to all those who believe in Him as the revealer of the pure life of God the Father. "These are they that come out of the great tribulation, and they washed their robes and made them white in the blood of the Lamb" (Rev. 7:14).

blood, spilling of—(see *meat eating*)

boat—Symbolizes a positive, sustaining state of consciousness that prevents one from sinking into a negative condition (water) and bears up the faculties of the mind.

body—The outer expression of consciousness; the precipitation of the thinking part of man. God created the idea of the body of man as a self-perpetuating, self-renewing organism, which man reconstructs into his personal body. God creates the body idea, or divine idea, and man, by his thinking, makes it manifest. As God created man in His image and likeness by the power of His word, so man, as God's image and likeness, projects his body by the same power.

All thoughts and ideas embody themselves according to their character. Material thoughts make a material body. Spiritual thoughts make a spiritual body.

body, disintegration of the, cause and remedy— The body disintegrates because generation after generation men have tried to bring forth after the wisdom of Satan instead of the wisdom of God. Jesus made the unity between the superconsciousness in the top brain and the life center, and by following His methods and identifying ourselves with His spiritual consciousness we may get back into our former spiritual estate in the Garden of Eden. "As in Adam all die, so also in Christ shall all be made alive" (I Cor. 15:22).

body, effects of sin and righteousness on the—The body is destroyed, made sick unto death by sin and ignorance; the body is made alive in Christ through understanding and righteousness. "The wages of sin is death; but the free gift of God is eternal life in Christ Jesus" (Rom. 6:23).

body, given benefit of salvation—The body receives the benefit of salvation through prayer and spiritual meditation. In this way the substance of Spirit is carried by living words of Truth into every part of the body, and its quickening power makes alive the whole organism.

body, how to make perfect—Man may have a perfect body and a perfect world when he understands and uses the perfect word, the complete word, the word that contains all the attributes of God. When the words of man are charged with a full understanding of Divine Mind and its inhering ideas and he consciously applies this knowledge in all his feeling, thinking, speaking, and living, he will be able to show forth a perfect body and a perfect world.

body, how transformed—The body is transformed by the renewing of the mind. By affirmation the mind lays hold of living words of Truth and builds them into mind and body. When we enter into and abide in the Son of God consciousness we have eternal life, and the body is transformed into pure flesh manifesting the perfection of Spirit.

body, natural forces of the—The natural forces of the body are eager to co-operate with man in manifesting a perfect body. Man must co-operate with them by obeying divine law.

body, redemption of the—The body is made and sustained by thought. Its character is like the thought that made it. Every thought has in it an idea of substance and life. When the mind of man is in conscious union with Divine Mind his body manifests perfection.

The body can be redeemed only by man's taking it beyond the three dimensions of the earthly realm and raising it to the fourth dimension. The earthly body is substance in its gross form and as such is still subject to the physical laws that operate in gross substance. But when perfect ideas of life and substance are attained in consciousness, the three dimensions of mind, idea, and expression will be embraced in the fourth dimension of realization or Divine Mind. Then the same spiritual conditions will be found in manifestation as are in Spirit or God-Mind.

body, spiritual—The perfect manifestation of a divine idea. It is composed of spiritual substance so pure that no disintegrating force can be found in it. This body of pure Spirit is the very temple of the living God; a radiant, beautiful body illumined with the eternal light of Spirit. "That they may behold my glory, which thou hast given me" (John 17:24).

body of Christ—The body that is the result of spiritual thought. It maintains its unity with Spirit, even in manifestation. This is first individual, and then universal, including all men.

body of Christ, members of the—All those who forsake everything pertaining to the personal, limited self and measure up to the Christ standard in thoughts and acts, thus bringing forth the unlimited fruits of Spirit, are members of the one body: the body of Christ.

body of light—Jesus, dwelling continually in the consciousness of Being, the very substance and life of God, had conscious realization of His actual oneness with Spirit. His body became a "body . . . of light" (Luke 11: 34) spiritual substance, the very essence of Being. "He that hath seen me hath seen the Father" (John 14:9).

bondage—Undue attachment to thoughts in personal consciousness, such as race, class, sex, age, or personality. "Whatsoever thou shalt bind on earth shall be bound in heaven and whatsoever thou shalt loose on earth shall be loosed in heaven" (Matt. 16:19).

bosom, Abraham's—The peace and contentment that come to those who trust God.

bounty, the Lord's—The generosity of God.

bread—Representative of universal substance. The substance of the omnipresent Christ body. Our daily bread is the sustenance for spirit, mind, and body. Some of this daily bread is appropriated in the form of food. There is substance in words of Truth, and this substance is appropriated by prayer and meditation on Truth.

bread, breaking of—Stirring into action, in consciousness, of the inner substance of Spirit (bread) and the concentrating of mind on it as the real possession. "And they continued stedfastly in the apostles' teaching and fellowship, in the breaking of bread and the prayers" (Acts 2:42).

bread from heaven—Descent into man's consciousness of ideas that are manifested as manna, which feeds and refreshes. "I have meat to eat that ye know not" (John 4:32).

bread of life—The word of Truth that imparts new vitality to mind and body. "Thou shalt eat bread at my table continually" (II Sam. 9:7).

breastplate—The breastplate of the high priest of Israel had on it twelve precious stones, representing the twelve tribes of Israel. This means that the twelve faculties of the mind must be massed at the great brain center called the solar plexus.

breath—The inner life flow that pulsates through the whole being. The breathing of the manifest man corresponds to the inspiration of the spiritual man. When any man is inspired with high ideas he breathes "into his nostrils the breath of life" (Gen. 2:7).

breath of the Almighty—The inspiration of Spirit; the silent movement of God within our being.
"There is a spirit in man,
And the breath of the Almighty giveth them understanding"
(Job 32:8).

The breath of God, which became the soul of the man manifestation, includes all emotions and energies that move in and through the organism, and it is always designated as feminine. Psyche is the name of that subtle essence that flows in and out of the great heart center called in physiology the cardiac plexus. The name *Psyche,* which figures in Greek mythology, means breath, life. Psyche is represented as one of the three daughters of a king. These three "daughters" are spirit, soul, and body. Psyche is the soul in its many earthly experiences, in its failures and its successes.

breathing—The symbol of inspiration. Jesus breathed on His apostles and said to them, "Receive ye the Holy Spirit" (John 20:22).

brotherhood—An established thought in high spiritual consciousness. This thought springs from the understanding that God is the one Father and that all men are brothers.

burdens—Beliefs in ill-health, lack, personal responsibility, prejudice, fear, condemnation, and all other negative things. Truth will make us free from each one of these burdens.

burning bush—When we arrive at a four-sided or balanced state of mind, the light of intuition or flame of fire burns in our heart, yet it is not consumed; there is no loss of substance. In thinking there is a vibratory process in the brain that uses up nerve tissue, but in the wisdom that comes from the heart the "bush" or tissue is not consumed. This thinking in wisdom is "holy ground," or substance in its spiritual wholeness; that is, the idea of substance in Divine Mind.

by night—In the darkness of intellectual consciousness. Nicodemus visited with Jesus "by night" (John 3:2).

C

calf of gold—Represents the tendency of man to form images after the pattern that he sees with the eye rather than from the ideals that rise in the silent meditations of the mind.

Calvary—(see *Golgotha*)

camel—In individual consciousness the camel is a symbol of power, endurance, strength, and patient perseverance.

candlestick—The candlestick of the Temple represents the intelligence in man. The "seven golden candlesticks" of Rev. 1:12 are receptacles of spiritual light.

capacity, spiritual—Transcending intellectual knowledge. Nearly everyone has at some time touched this hidden wisdom and been more or less astonished at its revelations.

cause and effect—The law of sequence; the balance wheel of the universe. This law, like all other divine laws, inheres in Being and is good. "Whatsoever a man soweth, that shall he also reap" (Gal. 6:7). Man lives in two worlds, the world of cause (the within) and the world of effect (the without).

causes, primal—Primal causes are complete, finished, absolute. All that man manifests has its origin in a cause that we name Divine Mind. The one Mind is absolute, and all its manifestations or effects are in essence like itself. This being true in logic, it is not a difficult matter to arrive at the conclusion that the effect proves the character of the cause.

cells of the body—Structural and functional units of organism made up of atoms composed of electrons and protons, which, in reality, have their origin in the super-mind.

These cells are adjusted one to the other through associated ideas. When divine love enters into man's thought process every cell is poised and balanced in right order. Law and order rule in the cells of the body with the exactness that characterizes their action in the worlds of a planetary system.

center in consciousness—A faculty through which a mind quality is expressed. When a center loses its power it should be baptized by the word of Spirit. This cleanses all material thought; impotence is vitalized with new life, and the whole subconsciousness is awakened and quickened.

chaos—Disorder; confusion; discord. Chaos in body and affairs results from chaos in mind, a product of the sense man.

character, spiritual—The true estimate of man's qualities. Character building is ever from within outward. Spiritual discernment of the reality of man's origin and being in God is the only enduring foundation of character.

cheerfulness—A steady, quiet, beautiful expression of the joy of God. It is conducive to good health because it frees one from tension.

chemicalization—A condition in the mind that is brought about by the conflict that takes place when a high spiritual realization contacts an old error state of consciousness.

The mind of man is constantly at work, and this work results in the production of thought forms. These thought forms assume individual definiteness; they take on personality, which works out into the body. Whenever a new spiritual idea is introduced into the mind, some negative belief is disturbed. It resists. With this resistance comes more or less commotion in the consciousness. This is called chemicalization. This can be greatly modified or eliminated by putting the mind in divine order through denial.

If the cleansing baptism of denial does not precede the Holy Spirit's descent, there is conflict in the consciousness—the old error thoughts contend for their place, refuse to go out, and a veritable war is the result. When the conscious mind has been put in order, the Holy Spirit descends with peace like a dove.

cherubim—Protection; sacred life. The inner, spiritual life is protected from the outer, coarser consciousness. The cherubim spread their wings over the place of the Ark and covered it. Also in the Scriptures cherubim are symbolic figures representing the attributes and majesty of God.

childlike—(see *meek*)

Children of Israel—The thoughts of reality or the true ideas about Being that have to be brought out in every part of man's consciousness. These thoughts are brought down from the land of Canaan into Egypt (the flesh consciousness) and, for a season, are submerged in the fleshly realm, or thoughts in form.

Heaven, according to Jesus, is within man; and with this understanding we see that the escape of the Israelites from Egypt is paralleled by the escape of man from ignorance and materiality.

chosen of God—God has chosen each of us as a medium for the expression of Himself as love, life, wisdom, abundance, health, and so forth. "Ye did not choose me, but I chose you, and appointed you, that ye should go and bear fruit" (John 15:16).

chosen people—The "royal priesthood" making up the Christ body; by overcoming, they have incorporated into their consciousness the attributes of God. They are the living expression of His righteousness and glory.

Christ—The incarnating principle of the God-man; the perfect Word or idea of God, which unfolds into the true man and is blessed with eternal life by measuring up to the divine standard, thus fulfilling the law of righteousness. "Thou art my beloved Son, in thee I am well pleased" (Mark 1:11).

Christ is the divine man. Jesus is the name that represents an individual expression of the Christ idea. Christ existed long before Jesus. It was the Christ Mind in Jesus that exclaimed, "And now, Father, glorify thou me with thine own self with the glory which I had with thee before the world was" (John 17:5).

Christ abides in each person as his potential perfection. Jesus Christ, the embodiment of all divine ideas, exists eternally in the Mind of Being as the only begotten Son of God, the "Messiah" or "anointed one," and is the living Principle working in man.

Christ and Jehovah—Jehovah of the Old Testament is the I AM, or Christ of God invisible; the Messiah is the promise of the visible manifestation of that I AM, or Christ, and Jesus Christ is the fulfillment in man of that original spiritual I AM, or Jehovah.

Christ, abide in—To dwell continually in the consciousness of Christ to the point of realization of unity with the Father and Son. To abide in Christ is to live in the perfection of God-Mind, the thought of God, the living Christ.

Christ, birth of—Man is the bringing forth (the birth) of God's idea of man, the Christ of God. This is done through the quickening power of the word of Truth. The birth of Christ is the beginning in the inner realms of consciousness of a higher set of faculties, which, when grown to full stature, will save the whole man from ignorance, sickness, and death.

Christ, first coming of—The dawning in mind that spiritual man is the real Son of God.

Christ, formation of—When man appropriates words of Truth he partakes of that which forms the spiritual soul, substance, and life of Spirit and which manifests as Christ in the perfect body. Every student of Truth is letting "Christ be formed" (Gal. 4:19) in him when he constantly abides in the Christ Mind through daily meditating on words of Truth.

Christ, indwelling—The Son of God or spiritual nucleus within each person. All our thoughts must harmonize with this spiritual center before we can bring into expression the divine consciousness. Each man has within himself the Christ idea, just as Jesus had. Man must look to the indwelling Christ in order to recognize his sonship, his divine origin and birth, even as did the Saviour. This real self is "closer . . . than breathing, and nearer than hands and feet." It is the kingdom of God in each person. "Neither shall they say, Lo, here! or, There! for lo, the kingdom of God is within you" (Luke 17:21).

Christ in you—The true light, which guides every man coming into the world, is, and ever has been, in man. Even the outer man was formed and came into existence through it. This is "Christ in you, the hope of glory" (Col. 1:27).

Christ, joint heirs with—We are joint heirs with Christ to all that the Father has. This truth alone—the belief that in the regenerate state we are to be like Jesus, who became Christ manifested—leads us to a desire and an effort to attain our inheritance of eternal life here and now, because we know that there is no other thing in the universe worth striving for.

Christ, second coming of—The awakening and the regeneration of the subconscious mind through the super-conscious or Christ Mind.

Christ body, work of the—The work of the Christ body is the "restoration of all things, whereof God spake by the mouth of his holy prophets that have been from of old" (Acts 3:21). (see *body of Christ*)

Christian conversion—A letting go of sin; a moral cleansing. This type of conversion is good as far as it goes, but it is far from complete. (see *conversion*)

Christianity—The science of eternal life. It is governed by scientific principles of mind action, which are really the foundation of all the various sciences.

Christianity began with Jesus and was carried on by His apostles. He commanded them to cast out demons, to heal the sick, to make the blind to see, even to raise the dead. Whenever Truth is declared in the name of Jesus Christ, the demons of fear and disease are cast out.

Christianity, esoteric—Christianity that deals with the deep metaphysical truths that Jesus taught. "The letter killeth, but the spirit giveth life" (II Cor. 3:6).

Christianity, exoteric—Christianity that deals with the letter or surface meaning of the teachings of Jesus.

Christianity, practical—The teachings of Jesus practically applied to the everyday life of man. Practical Christianity is not a term applied to an arbitrary theory of human origin; neither is it a revelation to humanity from some prophet whose word alone must be taken unquestionably as authority. It is, in this respect, different from most religious systems of the world. Its students are not asked to believe anything that they cannot logically demonstrate to be true. Thus, it is the only system of religion before the people today that, because of its universal appeal to the pure reason in man, can be accepted and applied by every nation under the sun.

Christian, or Gentile—In the New Testament symbology Christian typifies the spiritual and Gentile the material.

church—The word *church* is derived from a Greek word meaning "the Lord's house." The individual's consciousness is his "Lord's house," and assembled within it are groups or aggregations of ideas (thought centers). The spiritualized will carries to the different "churches" (thought centers) the word of Truth and builds them up into a knowledge of their perfection and divinity by training them in spiritual thinking.

church of Christ—Spiritual consciousness, first individual, then collective. In the general usage the word *church* applies to persons who have been "born anew" (John 3:3) through the quickening power of the word, gathered together in one body, their union being typified by the human body.

Jesus never organized a church on earth; neither did He authorize anyone else to do so. He said to Peter, "Upon this rock I will build my church" (Matt. 16:18). He did not tell Peter that he was to be the head of the church, with a line of popes to follow. He said, "I will build my church" (ecclesia, assembly, or called-out ones). Jesus is still the head of His "assembly," and its only organization is in Spirit. He gave but one guide, one source from which His followers should receive their inspiration: "The Holy Spirit, whom the Father will send in my name, he shall teach you all things, and bring to your remembrance all that I said unto you" (John 14:26).

circulation, spiritual—The inner stream of life, substance, and intelligence flowing freely through the entire being.

circumcision—Symbolical of the cutting off of mortal tendencies; indicative of purification and cleanliness under divine law. Circumcision is fulfilled in its spiritual meaning by the freeing of the individual from the law of sin and death. "Circumcision is that of the heart, in the spirit not in the letter" (Rom. 2:29).

clairvoyance—"The power of discerning objects not present to the senses but regarded as having objective reality" (Webster). Intuitive perception; clear vision. Everything that takes place in the world of manifestation first takes place in the realm of thought. If one is spiritually quickened to the measure that he can discern the thought movements, he can gain a foreknowledge of what is about to occur.

coats of skins—The body of flesh. Man was connected originally with the spiritual-body idea, but when he took on personal consciousness he was given "coats of skins," which, under divine law, corresponded with the quality of his thought world. When spiritual thought becomes supreme in consciousness, the coats of skins will give way to the manifestation of the spiritual body, which is the immortal body that was spoken of by Paul.

coat without seam—The "coat . . . without seam," which the soldiers did not separate, represents the great unified doctrine of Truth that Jesus left (John 19:23).

cocreator, man with God—"My Father worketh even until now, and I work" (John 5:17). God creates in the ideal, and man carries out in the manifest world what God has idealized. Jesus treats this relation between the Father and the Son in the 5th chapter of The Gospel According to John: "The Son can do nothing of himself, but what he seeth the Father doing: for what things soever he doeth, the Son also doeth in like manner" (John 5:19).

Comforter, the—The Holy Spirit, the only authorized interpreter of the gospel of Jesus; He who gives comfort and cheer and reveals the Truth of God to us.

commandments—Having to do with the law or the orderly working out of divine principles. Moses represents the "Thou shalt not" phase of law; Jesus represents the "Thou shalt" phase of law.

commandments, to keep His—This is to command, to control, and to direct every thought according to the harmonious law of love one to another.

communion—Sharing the deep aspirations of our heart with the indwelling Father and hearing His "still small voice" (I Kings 19:12).

communion, kept secret—There are times when it is to our own spiritual benefit and to God's glory to keep things concealed and, like Mary, to ponder them in our heart until due time for expression. There are joys of the Spirit that are secret between a man and his Lord. One feels a sense of condemnation and depletion if he talks too freely about his communion with the Lord.

companionship—Association of those who are in divine harmony. This perfect fellowship is best found by those who practice quiet communion with God.

compass, points of the—In scriptural symbology east means the within, which is spiritual; west, the without, which is expression; north, the above, or intellect; south, the below, or physical.

compassion, divine—In the heart of God exists an eternal tenderness and mercy for His children. "Jehovah is gracious, and merciful" (Psalms 145:8).

compassion, human—A characteristic of love and mercy prompted by an understanding heart. A compassionate mind sees the error, but does not condemn. "Neither do I condemn thee: go thy way; from henceforth sin no more" (John 8:11).

compensation, law of—The order under which one receives just remuneration. The law of compensation is universal and not subject to personal demands. If the mind is turned toward man as one's recompense, it is turned away from divine law.

concentration—A thought center; a nucleus of faith or spiritual confidence. The centering of the attention on a particular idea. Concentration forms a mental loadstone in the mind to which thought substance rushes like iron filings to a magnet, bringing the forces, whether mental or physical, to a common purpose.

conception—Power of forming ideas in substance; the embodiment of an idea.

condemnation, dangerous—According to Webster, *condemn* means "to pronounce to be wrong." There is always a cause for every mental tangent, and that which would kill the sense man, root and branch, has its point of departure from the line of harmony in the thought of condemnation. In John the Baptist it seemed a virtue, in that he condemned his own errors, but this led to his condemnation of Herod, through which action he lost his life. We are to learn from this that condemnation is a dangerous practice.

conditions, evil—In Divine Mind there is no recognition of evil conditions. Such conditions have no basis of reality. To rid ourselves of any appearance of evil, let us change our thought at once and begin to build a consciousness that knows nothing but good. Let us affirm: *"I am a child of the Absolute. God is good, and I am His perfect child. Everything that comes into my life is good."*

conqueror—Metaphysically, one who attains mastery over sense consciousness. "We are more than conquerors through him that loved us" (Rom. 8:37).

conscience—There is a divine goodness at the root of all existence. It is not necessary to give in detail the place of abode of each sentient part of this central goodness, for it is there, wherever you look, and whenever you look. No man is so lowly but that at the touch of its secret spring this divine goodness may be brought to light in him. This goodness sleeps in the recesses of every mind and comes forth when least expected. Many stifle it for years, maybe for ages, but eventually its day comes, and there is a day of reckoning. This is the law of universal balance—the equilibrium of Being. It cannot be put aside with transcendental philosophies or metaphysical denials any more than it can be smothered in the forces of the blind passions.

Whoever has felt the prick of conscience has been spoken to by the Holy Spirit. Whoever has sat at the feet of his own inner convictions has been aware of God's presence.

conscience, accusing—A state of mind that refuses to remit past sins and keeps one in a state of self-condemnation and remorse.

conscious mind—The mind that makes one know of one's mental operations and states of consciousness; that phase of mind in which one is actively aware of one's thoughts. The mind through which man establishes his identity.

consciousness—The sense of awareness, of knowing. The knowledge or realization of any idea, object, or condition. The sum total of all ideas accumulated in and affecting man's present being. The composite of ideas, thoughts, emotions, sensation, and knowledge that makes up the conscious, subconscious, and superconscious phases of mind. It includes all that man is aware of—spirit, soul, and body.

It is very important to understand the importance of our consciousness in spiritual growth. Divine ideas must be incorporated into our consciousness before they can mean anything to us. An intellectual concept does not suffice. To be satisfied with an intellectual understanding leaves us subject to sin, sickness, poverty, and death. To assure continuity of spirit, soul, and body as a whole, we must ever seek to incorporate divine ideas into our mind. A consciousness of eternal life places one in the stream of life that never fails.

consciousness, ascend in—Rise to the spiritual realms of mind.

consciousness, body—The subconscious mind in its work in the body—repairing, renewing, and conducting the functions of the body in harmony and health if right ideas are given to it, or disintegrating the organism and producing inharmonious action of the functions if untrue thoughts are sown in the mind.

consciousness, centers of—The subconscious realm in man has twelve great centers of action. Each of these twelve centers has control of a certain function in mind and body. The twelve centers are: faith, strength, judgment, love, power, imagination, understanding, will, order, zeal, renunciation (or elimination), and life.

consciousness, Christ—Consciousness built in accordance with the Christ ideal, or in absolute relationship to the Father. The perfect mind that was in Christ Jesus.

consciousness, illumined—A mind purified by the light of Truth.

consciousness, inner—The realm of the supermind as contrasted with the outer or conscious mind.

consciousness, material—A state of mind based on belief in the reality of materiality, or things as they appear. It is carnal mind expressing its unbelief in the omnipresence of God.

consciousness, negative—A mind filled with un-Godlike thoughts, such as fear, hate, greed, lust, resentments, discouragement, sickness, and poverty.

consciousness, positive—A mind filled with God's thoughts, such as power, strength, generosity, purity, and optimism.

consciousness, sense—A mental state that believes in and acts through the senses. To rise out of sense consciousness, we determine to return to conscious oneness with God. "I will arise and go to my Father" (Luke 15: 18).

consciousness, Son of God—A state of mind that is conscious of God's ideal man.

consciousness, spiritual—(see *Christ consciousness*)

consciousness, total—Conscious, subconscious, and superconscious phases of mind working as a whole, as a unit.

consecration—The dedication of one's everyday thought to God; a complete surrender of oneself to God. The entire mind is brought under the control of the Christ consciousness with whole-souled devotion to spiritual ideas. It is the one way to perfect peace of mind. Consecration also means the application of all one's tact, skill, and inspiration to bringing other men into the Christ light. Thus, the whole world is to be brought into the Christ fold and transformed by Truth. "Who then offereth willingly to consecrate himself this day unto Jehovah" (I Chron. 29:5).

contemplation—A form of meditation; a thought of becoming a child of God.

convalescence—That period during which pure life from on high is cleansing the consciousness, and the waters of negation are receding. The body does not always at a single bound regain its natural condition, but there is a gradual recovery.

conversion—"The experience associated with and involving a definite and decisive adoption of religion, especially a Christian religion" (Webster). Conversion is a change of heart and is a real experience, but it is merely introductory to the new life in Christ. When a person arrives at a certain exalted consciousness through the exercise of his mind in thinking about God and His laws, he is lifted above the thoughts of the world into a heavenly realm. This is the beginning of his entry into the kingdom of heaven. When man attains this high place in consciousness he is baptized by the Spirit; that is, his mind and even his body are suffused with spiritual essences, and he begins the process of becoming a new creature in Christ Jesus.

conviction—The state of being convinced. Metaphysically, it is the divine assurance that comes to one when he is fully satisfied of the worth of Truth. Conviction refuses to be influenced by the senses because it is founded in spiritual thought.

cords, scourge of—The specific statement of denial. General denial cleanses the consciousness, but secret sins may yet lurk in the inner parts. Small definite statements that cut into them like whipcords will erase these specific transgressions. "And he made a scourge of cords, and cast all out of the temple, both the sheep and the oxen" (John 2:15).

corruptible—The corruptible body is that which is subject to decay. When it is transformed into the spiritual body, it becomes incorruptible and is forever enduring. "This corruptible must put on incorruption" (I Cor. 15: 53).

cosmos—Order; system; harmony; the opposite of chaos. The universe is a cosmos because it expresses Divine Mind, the essence of all harmony and order.

country, far—A state of consciousness in which man has separated himself from an intimate spiritual association with the Father and thereby does not have the benefit of divine wisdom in his affairs.

courage—A spiritual quality that enables one to remain poised and centered in God amidst great difficulties and danger. The realization that the almighty God of the universe is a spiritual presence which is constantly striving to express in and through us fills us with new courage and a fearlessness that is beyond description. "Be strong, and let your heart take courage" (Psalms 31:24).

covenant—A solemn agreement or compact between two or more parties. "My covenant shall stand fast with him" (Psalms 89:28).

covenant, new—Jesus established a new and higher

consciousness for man and taught and practiced the truth
of the inner kingdom. This teaching is known as the
"new covenant" (Heb. 12:24). The new covenant is to
be written in the heart of each person.

Covenant, Ark of the—(see *Ark of the Covenant*)

covetousness—Insatiable desire to possess that which
belongs to another. Covetousness has no wisdom. When a
man gives up to its demands he does foolish things to
gain possession of the coveted object. "Thou shalt not
covet" (Exod. 20:17). (see *acquisitiveness*)

creation—The original plan of an idea in Spirit. Back
of the visible universe are both the original creative ideas
and those that are brought forth as earthly things. In
the creative process Divine Mind first ideates itself. In
the Scriptures this idea is named Jehovah, meaning I AM
the ever living—He who is eternal. The creation is carried
forward through the activity of the Holy Spirit.

The order of creation is from the formless to the
formed, from the invisible to the visible. This goes on
perpetually, and there is never a beginning or an ending
to the process. The ideal is continually pouring itself into
its creation and lifting it higher and yet higher. Apart
from mind nothing can be done. Man, in his forming and
bringing things into manifestation, uses the same creative
process in mind that God uses. First is mind; then the idea
in mind; then the materialization of the idea.

creation, described in Genesis—The 1st chapter of
Genesis describes the creative action of universal Mind
in the realm of ideas and does not pertain to the manifest world. This truth is substantiated in the 2d chapter,
where it is stated that there was not a man to till the soil.
This proves conclusively that the first creation described
is in the realm of ideas.

(The account of creation rendered by Ferrar Fenton
gives an enlightening translation from the Hebrew: "By
periods God created that which produced the Suns; then

that which produced the Earth" [Gen. 1:1]. This is in line with Truth.)

creative force in man—Spirit-mind is the creative force constantly working in man and all other creation. Those who fail to recognize Spirit-mind shining within them dwell in a continuous state of darkness and ignorance. To them the almighty Christ is nonexistent. "And the light shineth in the darkness; and the darkness apprehended it not" (John 1:5).

creative intelligence—Mind of God forever upbuilding His universe.

creative Principle—God as the cause and moving force in and through all creation.

Cross—The Cross represents that state of consciousness termed "mortal mind." This is the "carnal mind" of Paul also, and it burdens the body with its various erroneous beliefs. "He went out, bearing the cross for himself" (John 19:17). The center of action of this "carnal mind" is in the brain, and it is here that it has to be met in the final overcoming that the I AM undertakes. "The place called The place of a skull" (John 19:17).

The Cross is not a burden as commonly understood, but a symbol of the forces in man adjusted in their right relation.

crown—That which imparts honor or splendor. Highest state or quality. The crown of eternal life is the prize to all who overcome carnal mind.

crucifixion—The crossing out in consciousness of errors that have become fixed states of mind; the surrender or death of the whole personality in order that the Christ Mind may be expressed in all its fullness.

The crucifixion of Jesus represents the wiping of personality out of consciousness. We deny the human self so that we may unite with the selfless. We give up the mortal so that we may attain the immortal. We dissolve the thought of the physical body so that we may realize the spiritual body.

cup—The consciousness of eternal life. This must be attained by an utter crossing out of the personal self. This is "the cup which the Father hath given me" (John 18:11).

curse—To affirm evil for or on something or someone. Cursing has a variety of meanings as used in the Scriptures. The whole human family is pictured as under the curse of God for not bringing forth spiritual good, because of disobedience and failure to observe divine law. "If ye will not hear, and if ye will not lay it to heart, to give glory unto my name, saith Jehovah of hosts, then will I send the curse upon you, and I will curse your blessings; yea, I have cursed them already, because ye do not lay it to heart" (Mal. 2:2).

God is love, and God's law of love cannot be broken. Man brings evil on himself by not obeying the law. Jesus redeemed mankind from the ancient curse of Jehovah, but men are themselves responsible for avoiding transgression of the law. "Christ redeemed us from the curse of the law" (Gal. 3:13).

D

dainties, king's—That which pertains to sensual gratification.

dark sayings—Refers to the darkened consciousness that cannot yet see the true light. Jesus knew that the apostles would soon reach the point where they would be able to go direct to the Father for light and guidance. Then He would not have to speak to them in "dark sayings" that they could not understand, but could speak to them "plainly of the Father" (John 16:25).

darkness—The ignorance of the sense man; the absence of Truth (light) in consciousness. Darkness represents undeveloped capacity. It is caused by lack of love. "He that saith he is in the light and hateth his brother, is in the darkness" (I John 2:9).

dawn—Spiritual perception as a dawning light in consciousness, increasing as one turns steadily toward Truth.

day—Represents the state of mind in which intelligence dominates. The idea back of day is light, or the dispensation of intelligence. In the Scriptures day and night are symbols for degrees of unfoldment, day being understanding; night, ignorance. (see *night*)

day, last—All shall attain who believe or have faith in the spiritual source of life. Whoever enters into the Mind of Spirit will have poured out to him its life essence and be wholly raised up from material conditions when arriving at the "last day"—the last degree of understanding.

day of judgment—Any day in which we get the result in body and affairs of some thought or word that we have expressed.

day of rest—The true day of rest is the consciousness of universal peace that constitutes the kingdom of heaven. This peace is eternal, and when man becomes conscious of it his "day of rest" has begun to dawn. This rest comes from the understanding that now in Christ all things are complete.

days, three—The three days that Jesus was in the tomb represent the three steps in overcoming error. First, nonresistance and humility; second, the taking on of divine activity, or accepting the will of God; third, the assimilation and fulfillment of divine will.

daydreamer—One having ideas brilliant beyond description, but which are not clothed in the habiliments of action. He perceives an idea, but does not give it form by infusing into it the substance of living faith. He falls short by failing to realize that there are two sides to every proposition, the image and the expression.

death—Physical dissolution of the body; the outer symbol of mental negation or spiritual inertia. As commonly interpreted, death is the absence of life in the body. Death is caused by man's failure to comply fully with God's law. It is the result of sin and has no uplifting power. A falling short of the law of life is sin. Sin causes discord in mind, which produces a separation between spirit and body. Through believing in error and dissipating the life substance, the mind loses hold of its consciousness of life and enters into negation, and dissolution takes place. The result is death of the body temple. "The wages of sin is death; but the free gift of God is eternal life" (Rom. 6:23).

If, through the power of our thought and word, we affirm the opposite of life and talk about the absence of life, we rob the body cells of their natural element. This treatment will eventually bring death to the organism. Let us not say, "I am tired"; "I am weak"; "I am sick." Rather, let us say, *"I am strong"; "I am well"; "I am alive with the life of God now and forevermore."*

death, an enemy of man—Death is not a friend but

an enemy and must be overcome. Death does not change man and bring him into the resurrection and eternal life. Death has no place in the Absolute.

In the world today there is an active effort to exalt death and to delude men into believing that death is the way to eternal life in heaven. Such a thought is opposed to the teachings of Jesus, because Jesus came to deliver the human race from death and to fulfill in man God's perfect will: abundant life. Jesus made no mention of resurrection after death as having any part in the new birth. The new birth is a change that comes here and now. It has to do with the present man, that he may become conscious of Christ within himself. Those who are guided by the Spirit of truth understand the life teaching and are not led astray by any philosophy that makes death and the grave necessary factors in spiritual growth.

death, a sleep—Death is but a prolonged sleep, the result of thought inharmony so great that the body cannot stand the strain and collapses. Then, instead of being in a body when he awakes, man finds that he is in the realm of thought without a vehicle adequate to his full expression, and he is forced by divine law again to build an organism.

death, first and second—The first death is the death of the light and life of Spirit in man's consciousness. The second death is a cessation of vital force and action in the body. It occurs when the mind completely loses control of the body. The functional activities cease, and the physical organism dissolves.

death, how to overcome—The Christ man goes through the various centers of the body and rebuilds them with his word. The abiding consciousness of life fills every cell of the body with its quickening energy, and the body becomes immortal.

debt—A contradiction of the universal equilibrium. There is no such thing as lack of equilibrium in all the universe; therefore, in Spirit and in Truth there is no debt.

Debts are produced by thoughts of lack, impatient desire, and covetousness. A thought of debt will produce debt. As long as we believe in debt, we shall go into debt and accumulate the burdens that follow this thought. When such thoughts are erased from consciousness, our debts are overcome and paid in full.

debt, how to overcome—Thoughts of abundance will more quickly and surely bring what is ours to us than any thoughts we can hold about debtors discharging their obligations to us. We are to see abundance everywhere and to affirm it, not only for ourselves but for everyone else. We shall fill our mind with thoughts of divine love, justice, peace, and forgiveness. This will pay our debts of love, which will bring to us abundance to meet every obligation.

decree—To command; to ordain. To decree with assurance is to establish and to fix an ideal in substance. The force behind the decree is invisible, like a promise to be fulfilled at a future time; but it binds with its invisible chains the one who makes it. We have only a slight conception of the strength of the intangible. We compare and measure strength by some strong element in nature. We say that something is as "strong as steel." But a little thought will convince us that mental affirmations are far stronger than the strongest visible thing in the world. The reason for this is that visible things lack livingness. They are not linked with energy and intelligence as are words. Words charged with power and intelligence increase with use, while material things decrease.

Deity, the—The Supreme Being; God.

delusion—False perception. Delusion occurs only in that realm which is not established by the divine Logos, God's creative Word.

demon—This word is used in Matt. 8:28-34, when

the demons ask to be sent into the swine. The demons of the parable represent error states of mind that have been quickened by Truth and are repentant. When one knows the work of Jesus in regenerating or reconstructing the mind and body and that this work is typical of what all have to do, one sees that negative thoughts have to be dealt with. One also understands that the demons or devils are error states of mind that have to be lifted up by the quickening power of Spirit. (see *Christianity* and *Devil*)

demonstrate—"To prove by reasoning, as by deduction; to establish as true" (Webster). To demonstrate Truth is to effect a change of consciousness. This includes the elimination of error and the establishment of Truth.

demonstration—The proving of a Truth principle in one's body or affairs. The manifestation of an ideal when its accomplishment has been brought about by one's conformity in thought, word, and act to the creative Principle of God.

It is a metaphysical law that there are three steps in every demonstration: the recognition of Truth as it is in Principle; holding an idea; and acknowledging fulfillment. "Whatsoever ye shall ask in prayer, believing, ye shall receive" (Matt. 21:22).

demonstration, complete—God expressed in all fullness; the putting on of Christhood, which Jesus accomplished.

demonstration, spiritual—A spiritual realization followed by the manifestation in the outer of the Truth that has been realized within.

demonstration, the great—That which crowns all others and includes all others—the demonstration of eternal life; the truth that life is omnipresent and eternal and that it is ours just to the measure that we appropriate it.

demonstrator—One who understands and conforms to any point of divine law. He may demonstrate much or little; he may deal with his whole consciousness or merely with his outer mentality. (see *overcomer*)

denial—The mental process of erasing from consciousness the false beliefs of the sense mind. Denial clears away belief in evil as reality and thus makes room for the establishing of Truth.

Carnal consciousness is made up of a multitude of false individual and race beliefs. Through denial we get rid of these shadows of reality. We cleanse the temple of the mind of these thieves and robbers of our good. In so doing, we make way for the planting of the seeds of Truth that will bring to us an ever-increasing supply of good. (see *affirmation*)

denials, as related to affirmations—A denial is a relinquishment, and it should not be made with too much vehemence. Let us make our denials as though we were gently sweeping away cobwebs, and our affirmations in a strong, bold, positive attitude of mind. When we poise ourselves in Divine Mind our affirmations and denials will be made in right relation. We will know just when to let go of a thought and when to lay hold of another.

deny himself—When a man denies himself he denies personality; he denies that the world of appearance is real. "If any man would come after me, let him deny himself . . . and follow me" (Mark 8:34).

desert place—A desert place in the consciousness of man is a seeming lack of substance and life. In Truth desert places do not really exist. From the viewpoint of Spirit there is no lack. Where God is, there are His inexhaustible resources; God is everywhere present.

desire—An expression of the inmost being of man; the onward impulse of an ever-evolving man. It springs from deep within Being and it has enduring power. Deep desire is essential to spiritual growth. It is desire—earnest, intense desire—that draws the whole being up out of mortality and its transient joys into the power to appreciate and to receive real spiritual blessings.

desire, repressed—Desire that is forced out of consciousness into the subconscious mind without transmutation according to spiritual law.

desire to excel—The inspiration of the Holy Spirit, which ever urges us to forsake earthly things and to desire that which is of heaven. Desire to excel should be encouraged and cultivated in the right direction. It is in all men.

destiny—The goal toward which man's own thoughts are leading him. In the beginning he was destined to bring forth God's perfect pattern and he must eventually reach this supreme goal. Man's destiny is to go from glory to glory.

development—Increase in conception and expression of the qualities that belong to Divine Mind. The development or correction of all present, ideas underlying one's manifestation, and the training of them to conform to the divine idea of man.

Devil—The mass of thoughts that has been built up in race consciousness through many generations of earthly experiences and crystallized into what may be termed human personality, or carnal mind, which opposes and rejects God.

The "devil" is a state of consciousness adverse to the divine good. Other names for this state of consciousness are *the Adversary, carnal mind, the accuser,* and *the old man.* There is no personal devil. God is the one omnipresent Principle of the universe, and there is no room for any principle of evil, personified or otherwise.

Devil, how to overcome the—The Devil is overcome by denying his existence and by affirming universal Christ love for God and all men. The devils that we encounter are fear, anger, jealousy, and other similar negative traits, and they are in ourselves. Christ gives us the power to cast out these devils, thereby cleansing our consciousness.

digestion, spiritual—Absorbing Truth into the consciousness through meditation.

discern—"To lay hold of with the understanding, especially that which is hidden or obscure; to divine" (Webster). To apprehend the Truth of Being; to look through appearances and to behold the reality of omnipresence.

discerning the Lord's body—(see I Cor. 11:29) To discern the Lord's body is to recognize that it is substance and life, and it is formed within man, and that it is, in the larger sense, made up of members in whom the Christ body has been individually formed.

discernment, spiritual—That inner spiritual faculty by which man may receive the revelations of God-Mind. The faculty by which we inwardly know that which is spiritual. It indicates the ready insight into divine law that was the glory of the Master.

disciple—"One who receives instruction from another" (Webster). (see *apostles*)

disciple, calling of—To call a disciple (or apostle) is mentally to recognize that disciple; it is to identify oneself with the intelligence working at a center: for example, judgment at the solar plexus. To make this identification, one must realize one's unity with God through Christ, Christ being the Son-of-God idea always existing in man's consciousness.

disciples in the upper room—The gathering of the disciples (or apostles) in the upper room symbolizes the concentration of the faculties at the center of spirituality in communion with the Father.

discrimination—The ability to distinguish qualities or values, enabling one intelligently to choose the desirable.

disease—An inharmonious condition in mind and body brought about by error thinking. Ignorance causes all disease. "My people are destroyed for lack of knowledge" (Hosea 4:6). Organic disease has its origin in mind as truly as any other manifestation. It has become subconscious and needs the power of the Christ Mind to reach and to dissolve the error thoughts that are causing the disease.

dispensation, new—The great outpouring of power, love, and spiritual life that is now taking place in all who acknowledge the I AM presence.

dispensation, old—The Mosaic dispensation.

divine—Godlike; godly; of the nature of God.

divine ideal—The Christ man; the divine idea of man.

divine law—The logical process by which Principle or God manifests.

Divine Mind—God-Mind; ever-present, all-knowing Mind; the Absolute, the unlimited. Omnipresent, all-wise, all-loving, all-powerful Spirit.

There is but one Mind, and that Mind cannot be separated or divided, because, like the principle of mathematics, it is indivisible. All that we can say of the one Mind is that it is absolute and that all its manifestations are in essence like itself.

Divine Mind, creative power of—The functioning of the principles of Being; Spirit in action. Mind is not a thing; Mind *is*. It is that which, through orderly processes, produces things. Divine Mind first conceives the idea, then images its fulfillment. Man, acting in co-operation with Divine Mind, places himself under this same creative law and thus brings his ideas into manifestation.

divine motherhood—The brooding, nourishing element of Divine Mind, in which spiritual ideas are brought to fruition.

divine order—Order is the first law of the universe. Indeed, there could be no universe unless its various parts were kept in perfect order. The facts of Spirit are of spiritual character and, when understood in their right relation, they are orderly. Orderliness is law and is the test of true science.

divinity within us—The true spiritual man, the Christ that is the real of every man.

doctrine of church—A teaching peculiar to a church or to churches in general.

doctrine of Unity, value of the—Unity doctrine is of practical, everyday value to everyone who follows its instructions because it shows man that he is his own minister, lawyer, and doctor and that he has within himself the storehouse from which he can supply every need. It is the doctrine that Jesus proclaimed with original simplicity. It asks man to return again to the estate of simplicity in which he was as a little child, believing implicitly what the Father tells him from the inner recesses of his own being. It has been found to be a good doctrine because it has opened to man a new world, and he sees how, through it, shall be brought about the fulfillment of the promise: "And he [God] shall wipe away every tear from their eyes; and death shall be no more; neither shall there be mourning, nor crying, nor pain, anymore: the first things are passed away" (Rev. 21:4).

domination—"Exercise of power in ruling; often, arbitrary or insolent sway" (Webster). One person should never dominate another because it weakens the will of the one dominated and makes the will of the one who dominates hard and unyielding.

dominion—"Supreme authority, sovereignty" (Webster). As a perfect child of God, man is born to complete dominion over all creation. Dominion is an inner consciousness obtained only through mind discipline. This supreme authority comes as man realizes his oneness with the Father.

dominion, urge to exercise—The power and right of dominion and authority are innate within man, having been implanted there by Divine Mind at man's creation.

door—The door of our mind is the I AM. "I am the door of the sheep" (John 10:7). The "sheep" are our thoughts. There is but one life-giver, one Saviour, the Christ; and the only door through which the divine essence can come to us is through our own I AM.

door of the temple—The "door of the temple which is called Beautiful" (Acts 3:2) is the way that opens to spiritual illumination, to an understanding of how to lay hold of and to apply spiritual law.

double-mindedness—Contemplation of a world both good and evil; mental acceptance of a principle of evil as well as of good. This constitutes a denial of God as omnipresent good.

doubt—"Unsettled state of opinion concerning the reality of the truth of something" (Webster). Doubt is the Satan of every man. Doubt is the root of weakness, mental and physical. If men had faith in themselves, in the ability of Spirit within them, they would become giants, where they are but pygmies.

dove—Symbolizes peace of mind and confidence in divine law. The dove is nonresistant. In this state of consciousness we rest in Spirit.

drink of the cup—To drink of the cup from which Jesus drank is to rise above all sensuality, to gain mastery over every impulse of mind and body, and to devote one's whole life to Spirit.

drunkard—"One who habitually drinks strong liquors immoderately" (Webster). The first step in healing the drunkard in ourselves or another is to withdraw all condemnation and censure and to affirm the law of love. There is a very close connection in Being between love and life.

A man once testified that he healed himself of drunkenness by saying, whenever the desire for liquor came to him, *"I do not love whisky; I love God."*

duality—(see *double-mindedness*)

dust, shake off the—To deny all seeming materiality. "And whosoever shall not receive you, nor hear your words, as ye go forth out of that house or that city, shake off the dust of your feet" (Matt. 10:14).

dying—The state of negation in man's consciousness wherein he is failing to retain possession of his body.

dying to self—Signifies man's willingness to die to the little personal self, so that he may be absorbed into Divine Mind. To lay down the mortal thought of life and to take up the spiritual idea of life opens the door to the realization that the I AM has creative power and can express the life manifestation in divine order.

E

ears—Represent the obedience and receptivity of the mind.

earth—Metaphysically speaking, the earth represents the consciousness of the physical body.

east—The within. As used in Matt. 2:1, the word in the original is plural; thus, from the regions of interior wisdom come thoughts of reverence and rich gifts of substance, understanding, and every spiritual help for the Christ child, whose growth in consciousness has begun.

Easter—The awakening and raising to spiritual consciousness of the I AM in man, which has been dead in trespasses and sins and buried in the tomb of materiality.

eat and drink—To appropriate; to become conscious of the food that "abideth unto eternal life," and to use it.

eat of the tree of life—The eternal life of God is within every man. When we consciously realize the presence of this life in every part of our organism we are eating of the tree of life.

eating—Eating is symbolical of mental appropriation of thoughts of substance. "Thy words were found, and I did eat them; and thy words were unto me a joy and the rejoicing of my heart" (Jer. 15:16).

Supplying the physical needs does not solve the whole problem of hunger for man, for his hungers are as varied as his interests and desires. They include his thoughts and feelings as well as his physical needs. When Jesus said, "He that eateth me, he also shall live because of me" (John 6:57), He referred to the appropriation of spiritual substance by man, and not to his eating of material food. We "eat" spiritual things when we affirm that we are strengthened and sustained by spiritual substance.

When in the holy silence you nourish your consciousness on God's word, you are eating of the "hidden manna" (Rev. 2:17), the bread that gives everlasting life. The Lord's Supper (Matt. 26:26-31) is a mental feast.

eating of the tree of good and evil—Appropriating the consciousness of both good and evil.

To "eat" is to appropriate the substance of ideas through thinking about them. "Evil" represents error-thought combinations; that part of consciousness which has lost sight of true principles and through sensation becomes enamored of the thing formed. Form has its place in creation, but it is subject to the creative idea that begets it. The activity of an idea in man's mind produces sensation. To become involved in the sensation of an idea to the exclusion of control is to eat of the "tree of the knowledge of good and evil" and to die to all consciousness of the original idea.

ecclesia—The church of Jesus Christ: the called-out ones.

Eden, Garden of—Represents a region of Being in which are provided all primal ideas for the production of the beautiful. As described in Genesis, it represents, allegorically, the elemental life and intelligence placed at the disposal of man and through which he is to evolve both mind and body.

The human body with its psychical and spiritual attributes comprises a miniature Garden of Eden. When man develops spiritual insight and in thought, word, and act voluntarily operates in accord with divine law, then rulership, authority, and dominion become his in both mind and body. "The kingdom of God is within you" (Luke 17:21). (see *Garden of Eden*)

education, spiritual—To draw forth from within, through meditation and prayer, the deep truths of God.

ego—The I. The ego is man, and by reason of his divinity he makes and remakes as he wills. In this lie his greatest strength and his greatest weakness. The ego of itself is possessed of nothing. It is a mere ignorant child of innocence floating in the Mind of Being, but through the door of its consciousness must pass all the treasures of God.

ego, adverse—When the ego attaches itself to sense consciousness, it builds the antichrist man, who has no basis in reality. This is known as the adverse ego. It is the adverse ego that causes all the trouble in the world. Its selfishness and greed make men grovel in the mire of materiality, when they might soar in the heavens of spirituality.

ego, spiritual—The true self; an individualized center of God consciousness; I AM; conscious identity.

egotism—A state of consciousness built up by the will functioning in the sense world. In this false expression it looks upon itself as great, honorable, mighty. Supreme egotism stops the flow of spiritual life in the organism, and body atrophy sets in.

Egypt—Mental bondage to sense thoughts; material consciousness. It pertains to the physical sense of life, the corporeal organism.

elimination—(see *renunciation*)

Elohim God—The original Mind in creative action. *El* means "the strong and ever-sustaining one," and *Alah,* "to swear or formulate by the power of the Word." Elohim thus represents the universal Principle of Being that designed all creation.

El Shaddai—(see *almighty*)

emanate—"To issue forth from a source" (Webster). In metaphysics, emanation usually refers to the silent influence of Mind of Spirit.

emotion—Undisciplined or uncontrolled forces. Subnormal or supernormal activity of mental or physical forces. Excitement of the feelings.

It is found that for each bad emotion there is a corresponding chemical change in the tissues of the body that is life-depressing and poisonous. Contrariwise, every good emotion makes a life-promoting change. Thus, it follows that it pays to think good thoughts and to do good acts for one's own sake.

"end of the world"—Literally, "the completion of this eon." This does not refer to the physical world, but to the present era or age; or individually, to the end of a certain state of consciousness.

The "end of the world" is the separation of the true from the false in consciousness, when the wisdom and understanding of Spirit are so developed in us that we, of our own accord, choose whom we will serve and select that which is right in the sight of God. "The world passeth away, and the lust thereof" (I John 2:17).

"The end of the world" is sometimes translated "the End of the Age" ("Emphatic Diaglott"), thus giving a clearer meaning to the text. The world, the age, the old order of things shall come to an end and pass away; and the new world, the new age, "wherein dwelleth righteousness," will be established.

energy—The power of God within us to accomplish. Strength or vigor of expression. Internal or inherent power, as of the mind; capacity of acting, or producing an effect.

Power forcibly exerted; force or action. Zeal in motion, the forerunner of every effect.

enthusiasm—"Ardent zeal or interest; fervor. Divine inspiration or possession" (Webster). It is a powerful expression of a living interest; it is active and vital. Enthusiasm is another word for zeal, and zeal is a great stimulator of man. You cannot think of or repeat the word *zeal* without evoking a certain mental thrill that spurs you to action in some direction.

entity—"A thing which has reality and distinctness of being either in fact or for thought" (Webster).

entities, protective—The shepherds who were watching their flocks by night at the time of Jesus' birth symbolize protective entities of God that have kept watch over the soul in its sleep between incarnations.

environment—Surroundings. Our consciousness is our real environment. The outer environment is always in correspondence to the thoughts making up our consciousness.

"Thou hast made the Most High thy habitation;
There shall no evil befall thee"
(Psalms 91:9, 10).

equivalent—"Equal in force or authority" (Webster). Our demonstrations are equivalent to the power and illumination contained in our realizations. We receive according to our capacity to receive.

error—That which is untrue. Error thoughts represent belief in thoughts and beliefs not of God. Error thoughts have no foundation in Truth. They originate in the intellect. They are eliminated by one's denying their reality and power, and affirming the Truth of Being.

essence, spiritual—The substance in which all things exist and out of which all things are made.

eternal—Without beginning or end; timeless; everlasting in duration. "The eternal God is *thy* dwelling-place" (Deut. 33:27).

ether—The spiritual substance in which we live, move,

and have our being and out of which can be made whatever we desire. Some scientists teach that space is heavily charged with energies that would transform the earth if they could be controlled. Arthur Eddington says that about half the leading physicists assert that the ether exists and the other half deny its existence; but, in his words, "Both parties mean exactly the same thing, and are divided only by words."

One with spiritual understanding knows that the ether exists as an emanation of Mind and should not be confused in its limitations with matter. Its being is governed and sustained by ideas, and ideas have no physical dimensions.

evil—That which is not of God; unreality; error thought; a product of the fallen human consciousness; negation.

Evil is a parasite. It has no permanent life of itself; its whole existence depends on the life it borrows from its parent, and when its connection with the parent is severed nothing remains. In Divine Mind there is no recognition of evil conditions. Such conditions have no basis of reality. They are conjurations of a false consciousness. Apparent evil is the result of ignorance, and when Truth is presented the error disappears.

There is but one presence and one power, God omnipotent. But man has the privilege and freedom of using this power as he will. When he misuses it he brings about inharmonious conditions. These are called evil. Evil appears in the world because man is not in spiritual understanding. He has not learned that all is Mind; neither has he conformed to the law of Mind, with the result that inharmony appears in his body and affairs. He can do away with evil by learning rightly to use the one Power. If there were a power of evil, it could not be changed.

evil, overcoming—Evil must be overcome with good. We must dwell in the good so wholly that all the substance of our thoughts and our being is given over to the promotion of the good. This is a mental process in which all negation (evil) is denied, and creative, fearless affirmation of God's perfect good is steadfastly adhered to.

evolution—The development achieved by man working under spiritual law. It is the result of the development of ideas in mind. What we are is the result of the evolution of our consciousness, and this consciousness is the result of seed ideas sown in the mind. In the beginning, God implanted His perfect word—involved this seed word into each man. Evolution is the unfolding in consciousness of that which God involved in man in the beginning. (see *involution*)

evolution, spiritual—The unfolding of the Spirit of God into expression. The Christ or Son of God evolution in man is plainly taught in the New Testament as the supreme attainment of every man. "For the earnest expectation of the creation waiteth for the revealing of the sons of God" (Rom. 8:19).

exaltation—A lifting up; a raising up of the consciousness in man from a physical and mental basis to the spiritual. Affirm: *"I hear the voice of God within me and I am exalted."*

exercise—The act of training the mind to think of God's attributes as forces that are being incorporated into the mind as one incorporates strength into the body. "Exercise thyself unto godliness" (I Tim. 4:7).

exercises, spiritual—Prayer, meditation, worship, and fasting from erroneous ideas.

existence—"State or fact of having being" (Webster); manifestation. The object of man's existence is to bring forth in the race that which exists in God.

exorcist—One who uses a holy name to cast out evil spirits; an imitator of Truth who is not in the understanding of the change of heart and thought that must accompany all true healing. (see Acts 19:13-16)

expectation—Anticipation of divine good. Looking

about for the wondrous benefits God has prepared for us.

In every person is that which causes him always to hope for and to expect that which is good and true. This very expectation helps the good to become active.

experimentation—Man is a free agent. He can open his mind to divine wisdom and know creative law, or he can work out his unfoldment through experimentation. Our race is in the experimental stage. In our ignorance we transgress the law to the very limit, and then a great reaction sets in, a general condition that is negative to the point of dissolution. Then, that in us which always looks obediently to God in an extremity is awakened, and we seek divine guidance.

external forms of religion, worship of—Undue attention to ritual and ceremony. Concern with the letter and not the spirit of religion.

eye, inner—Spiritual vision; intuitive seeing with the eye of Truth.

eye, single—Searching quality of mind with keen observation that selects only that which is good. The single eye is open and receptive only to the guiding light of Spirit.

eyes, blind—A darkened consciousness. When we are exalted and illumined through Truth darkness disappears. "And in that day shall the deaf hear the words of the book, and the eyes of the blind shall see out of obscurity and out of darkness" (Isa. 29:18).

F

faculty, spiritual—An individualized center of God consciousness. The twelve faculties or ideas in Divine Mind are: faith, strength, wisdom or judgment, love, power, imagination, understanding, will, order or law, zeal, renunciation, and life. Man takes control of his faculties through exercising the will.

There are two ways to develop the spiritual faculties: through the evolutionary law of experience and trial (the school of the twelve sons of Jacob); or by the direct power of the Word, or the I AM (the purifying of the twelve apostles of Jesus). The law of Moses and the experiences of the Children of Israel under the old dispensation represent the first; and the transforming power of the true Word, or gospel of Jesus Christ, as set forth in the New Testament, is the second. When Divine Mind is looked to as the one and only guide, the faculties of man are developed in an orderly manner through the power of the Word. "For sin shall not have dominion over you: for ye are not under law, but under grace" (Rom. 6:14).

faculties, awakened—Faculties of mind that have been expanded until they function in harmony with Divine Mind.

failure—Inability, through a lack of power, to make a demonstration. Seeming failure is often a steppingstone to something higher.

faintheartedness—Uncourageous thoughts, lacking ability and efficiency.

faith—The perceiving power of the mind linked with the power to shape substance. Spiritual assurance; the power to do the seemingly impossible. It is a magnetic power that draws unto us our heart's desire from the invisible spiritual substance. Faith is a deep inner knowing that that which is sought is already ours for the taking.

"Now faith is assurance of *things* hoped for" (Heb. 11:1).

A close analysis shows that faith is the foundation of all that man does. Jesus spoke of a new condition for the upliftment of the race. He called it the "kingdom of the heavens." He said it must be built upon the foundation typified by Peter (rock), who represents faith. This is proof that faith is closely related to the enduring, firm, unyielding forms of substance. The development of the faith faculty is a key to spiritual realization. "According to your faith be it done unto you" (Matt. 9:29).

Faith in God is the substance of existence. To have faith in God is to have the faith of God. We must have faith in God as our Father and source of all the good we desire.

Faith is more than mere belief. It is the very substance of that which is believed. It works by love. Thoughts of condemnation, enmity, and resistance must be released and divine love declared; then faith will work unhindered.

Faith working in spiritual substance accomplishes all things. This is the faith that co-operates with creative law. When faith is exercised deep in spiritual consciousness, it finds its abode; and under divine law, without variation or disappointment, it brings results that are seemingly miraculous.

faith, blind—An instinctive trust in a power higher than ourselves. Because blind faith does not understand the principles of Being, it is liable to discouragement and disappointment.

faith, center of—The pineal gland, located in the middle of the brain, is the center of faith in the body of man. Concentration of thought on this center opens the mind of man to spiritual faith.

faith compared with trust—Trust is a weaker brand of faith, but better than mistrust. As a rule, persons who merely trust the Lord do not understand divine law. If they had understanding, they would affirm the presence and power of God until the very substance of Spirit would appear in manifestation.

faith cure—Another name for spiritual healing.

faith, how cultivated—By studying the experiences of Peter (the apostle representing faith), we obtain suggestions on the development of this faculty. The vacillating allegiance of Peter to Jesus illustrates the growth of faith in one who has not developed this faculty. Faith is built up through denial of all doubt and fear and continuous affirmations of loyalty to the divine idea, the higher self. One must have faith in one's spiritual capacity and depend on it in the face of adverse appearances.

faith in oneself—The ground for man's faith in himself is the truth that he is a son of God and, as such, he inherits the divine nature. Man should have faith in himself because he cannot be successful in any line without such faith.

faith, intellectual—The faith that has its seat of action in the intellect only. Intellectual man has faith in his art, in his science, or in his philosophy, which answers his purpose for the time being.

faith of Jesus—Jesus did not claim an exclusive supernatural power, which we usually accredit to Him. He had explored the ether energy, which He called the "kingdom of the heavens"; His understanding was beyond that of the average man. However, He knew and said that other men could do what He did if they would only have faith. He encouraged His followers to take Him as a pattern for faith and to use the power of thought and word. Divine healing is due to the application of the same law that Jesus used. In most instances, He demanded faith on the part of those He healed; and with this faith as a point of mental and spiritual contact, He released the latent energy in the atomic structure of the ones in need of healing, and they were restored to life and health. "He that believeth on me, the works that I do shall he do also; and greater *works* than these shall he do" (John 14:12).

faith, prayer of—The act of mentally taking that which is desired. Jesus said, "All things whatsoever ye pray and ask for, believe that ye receive them, and ye shall have them" (Mark 11:24).

faith thinking—The most important power of man is the original faith-thinking faculty. All of us have the thinking faculty located in the head, from which we send forth good, bad, and indifferent thoughts. If we are educated and molded after the average pattern of the human family, we may live a lifetime and never have an original thought. The thinking faculty is supplied with the second-hand ideas of our ancestors, the dominant beliefs of the race, or the threadbare stock of the ordinary social swim. This is not faith thinking. Faith thinking is done only by one who has caught sight of the Truth of Being and who feeds his thinking faculty on images generated in the faith center. Faith thinking is not merely an intellectual process based on reasoning. The faith thinker does not compare, analyze, or draw conclusions from known premises. He does not take appearances into consideration; he is not biased by precedent. His thinking gives form, without cavil or question, to ideas that come straight from the eternal fount of wisdom. His perception impinges on the spiritual, and he knows.

faith, understanding—Faith that functions from Principle. It is based on knowledge of Truth. It understands the law of mind action; therefore, it has great strength. To know that certain causes produce certain results gives a bedrock foundation for faith.

faithless generation—A generation that lacks the spiritual faith and power to do the works Jesus would have it do, such as healing the sick and making the blind to see.

fall—A retrogression in consciousness from the pristine Christ Mind to the personal and sense mind of the Adam man.

false claims—Those who make the indwelling Spirit of truth their guide and authority will not be deceived by false claims made either by other persons or by institutions. The safe way is to trust the Spirit of truth continually for protection from false beliefs.

family, the Christ—Jesus said: "Who is my mother and my brethren? And looking round on them that sat round about him, he saith, Behold my mother and my brethren! For whosoever shall do the will of God, the same is my brother, and sister, and mother" (Mark 3:33-35).

family, the universal—If God is the Father of all, then all men and women are brothers and sisters in a universal family. In the Christ consciousness we are all one.

famine—Lack of faith in God's power to prosper.

fasting—Denial; abstinence from error thoughts, to the end that we may meditate on Truth and incorporate it into our consciousness of oneness with the Father.

fate—"That which is destined or decreed; appointed lot. Fate suggests inevitability and immutability in strict use, but usually carries no clear implication of whether it is good or evil" (Webster). Man, through his thought, is working out his own salvation; he is created in the image and likeness of God and is finally to reach "the goal unto the prize of the high calling of God in Christ Jesus" (Phil. 3:14).

Father—God through His Holy Spirit is the Father.

Father and Son—The Father-Mind is the living Principle, the Absolute, the Great Unlimited. The Son is the living Word.

Father and Son, result of knowing both—When we are quickened in spiritual understanding, we experience a renewal of mind and a transformation of body. The mortal becomes immortal, the corruptible becomes incorruptible. It is the resurrection into eternal life.

Father of lights—Source of profound understanding, illumination, wisdom. Through our realization of and meditation on spiritual illumination, we open the way for these spiritual gifts to be showered upon us.

Father-Principle—The exact and immutable Principle of Being, lying back of all existence as cause, and approachable only along lines of perfect law. It is omnipresent and is not subject to change or open to argument.

Father's house, the—The Christ consciousness. It is the center of man's consciousness and is made manifest to him by mind processes alone.

favor of God—Good realized through faithful obedience; the orderly unfoldment in mind and body that results from meditation and prayer; a blessing that comes to us through obedience to Spirit. The bringing about of an inner spiritual strength, resulting in the development of all parts of mind and body.

fear—"Painful emotion marked by alarm; dread; disquiet" (Webster). Fear is one of the most subtle and destructive errors that the carnal mind in man experiences. Fear is a paralyzer of mental action; it weakens both mind and body. Fear throws dust in our eyes and hides the mighty spiritual forces that are always with us. Blessed are those who deny ignorance and fear and affirm the presence and power of Spirit.

fear, how to overcome—Fear is cast out by perfect love. To know divine love is to be selfless, and to be selfless is to be without fear. The God-conscious person is filled with quietness and confidence.

fear of God—"Only fear Jehovah, and serve him in truth with all your heart" (I Sam. 12:24). In this scriptural passage the word *fear* is used with Webster's meaning: "Awe; profound reverence, especially for the Supreme Being."

fearfulness—State of mind that is full of fear. Fearfulness is a parasite; it drives away divine guidance and produces weakness of the heart.

feast—Appropriation in a large measure; that is, laying hold of divine potentialities.

feast in Jerusalem—A receptive state of mind toward all spiritual good. It is the realization of the unfailing substance of Divine Mind. A great peace is there—"the peace of God, which passeth all understanding (Phil. 4:7) —and a welling up of an indescribable substance that fills the whole being with satisfaction.

feast, marriage—Conscious union between spirit or mind and body in the silent influx of substance; the union of man with Spirit. A thirsting for things of Spirit is necessary before one can come to the spiritual marriage feast. Great desire for the light and purity of Spirit is the power that prepares man for this greatest of feasts. (see Matt. 22:1-15)

feast, Sabbath—The inflow of spiritual substance that we realize when we enter the silence.

feeding the five thousand—In the universal Mind is a substance that Jesus called the "Father," which is also the seed of all visible substance. It is the only real substance because it is unchangeable, while visible substance is in constant transition.

An idea is purely spiritual and can be apprehended only by the mind. It is never visible to the eye but can be sensed by man through any of his spiritual functions. When the attention has been centered on the idea of substance long enough and strongly enough, a consciousness of substance is generated; and, by the powers of the various faculties of the mind in right relation, visible substance is formed. In this way, Jesus brought into visibility the loaves and fishes to feed the five thousand.

feeling—Feeling is external to thought; behind every feeling or emotion there lies thought, which is its direct cause. To erase a feeling, a change of thought is required.

feet—Represent the phase of the understanding that connects us with the outer or manifest world and reveals the right relationship toward worldly conditions in general. We can take possession of all substance that we comprehend and understand, in the name of I AM. This is the meaning of Josh. 1:3: "Every place that the sole of your foot shall tread upon, to you have I given it, as I spake unto Moses."

feet, washing of—The denial of materiality is illustrated in Jesus' washing of the apostles' feet (John 13:5-10). Even Peter (who represents faith) must be cleansed from belief in the reality of material conditions. To wash another's feet seems a menial thing, but in this humble way Jesus taught and exemplified the willingness of divine love to serve, so that man may be redeemed from the pride of the flesh.

feminine—The divine feminine in man is the mother phase of Being. God, through His Holy Spirit, is the Father.

field—Outside the house of God. "He that soweth the good seed is the Son of man; and the field is the world" (Matt. 13:37-38).

fiery furnace—A state of mind in which one goes through a purifying process, and evil and error are destroyed.

fire—Symbolizes cleansing and purification, but it is more than a symbol. Material fire is the symbol, and the fire of Spirit is the reality. The whole universe is alive with a divine, living, spiritual energy that consumes all the dross of sense and materiality. It is a fire that burns eternally. Because this is true, some have assumed that disobedient, sinful persons are to live forever in everlasting torment. But if the fire is eternal, the dross is not, and when the error is consumed the burning stops. The fire consumes only when it meets anything un-

like itself. In purified man it is manifested as his eternal
life.

fire of God—The Word of God in action. It burns
out the dross of negative consciousness and reveals the
Christ.

fire, tongues of—Illumination of thought, in demonstration of Spirit's presence and power.

firmament—Faith in mind power, a firm, unwavering
place in consciousness. The firmament in the midst of
the waters is an idea of confidence or faith in the invisible.

first-born—The "first-born" of every state of consciousness is the personal *I*. When the flood of light
from the universal is let in through our declaration of
the one wisdom and one love, this *I* of every mortal state
of consciousness is slain, and there is a "great cry in
Egypt; for there was not a house where there was not one
dead" (Exod. 12:30).

fish—Represent ideas of multiplication and fecundity.
Accounts in which Jesus figures as a party to fish eating
are symbolical of the mental side of eating, which is the
appropriation of ideas.

The reason Jesus so often used fish to illustrate His
teaching is that He was a living demonstration of ideas,
and all that He did was in the realm of ideas rather than
in the realm of effects. Fish represent ideas in which
there is great possibility of increase; Jesus used these ideas
to represent the inexhaustible, everywhere present abundance.

fishers of men—Spiritually quickened men who are
strongly fortified in Truth and able to help others to find
the light.

flame of fire—Light of understanding that flames up
in the heart, yet does not consume substance. (see *burning
bush*)

flash of intelligence—The musical genius says he hears

the music in a flash and is often at his wit's end to tran-
scribe it fast enough. Many an immortal poem or prose
work has been flashed from the mind of the author without any apparent effort on his part. But if all the prayers
and mind efforts of literary geniuses were inquired into,
it would be found that there had been heroic mental
effort somewhere at some time. The realization of perfection takes root in the mind and may come forth in a
flash.

flesh—Mortal consciousness expressing itself through
appetite. It is overcome by denying that appetite is physical and by affirming it to be spiritual.

flesh, carnal or sensual—A malformation of the substance idea of Being. It must be transformed by right
conception of divine perfection before the mortal can put
on the immortal.

fleshpots of Egypt—The pleasures of sense.

flocks—Symbolical of thoughts. "Tend the flock of
God which is among you" (I Pet. 5:2).

food—A symbol of appropriation. Bread represents
the flesh; it is an outer form of the inner substance. (see
drink of the cup)

All food is primarily mental, and in the process of
digestion and assimilation it becomes part of the body
structure, making cells like itself in character. If we
wish to bring into manifestation the perfect spiritual body,
we should feed on words of Truth—foods that are spiritual in character—avoiding all that carry with them into
the system a mental atmosphere of sensuality, fear, or any
other discord.

foods, solid—The deeper truths that require much
study, meditation, prayer, and concentration in order that
they may be appropriated and assimilated by the mind.

food, spiritual—Thoughts and words of Truth; the
word of God.

"food which perisheth"—The race consciousness

strives for the things of sense, but one who has found the real substance and source of supply proclaims, "Work not for the food which perisheth, but for the food which abideth unto eternal life" (John 6:27).

forces, creative—Active physical or mental forces, having the capacity to produce or to create.

forehead—The seat of perception. The forehead is the center of consciousness, which the understanding of Truth seals; that is, it secretly unites the consciousness with Christ.

forerunner of Spirit—As symbolized by John the Baptist, the perception of Truth that prepares the way for Spirit through a letting go of old concepts and beliefs.

forgiveness—A process of giving up the false for the true; erasing sin and error from the mind and body. It is closely related to repentance, which is a turning from belief in sin to belief in God and righteousness. A sin is forgiven when one ceases to sin, and true forgiveness is only established through renewing the mind and body with thoughts and words of Truth.

Forgiveness really means the giving up of something. When you forgive yourself, you cease doing the things that you should not do. Jesus said that man has power to forgive sin. Sin is the falling short of divine law, and repentance and forgiveness are the only means that man has of getting out of sin and its effect and coming into harmony with the law.

It is through forgiveness that true spiritual healing is accomplished. Forgiveness removes the errors of the mind, and bodily harmony results in consonance with divine law.

The law is Truth, and Truth is all that is good. There is no power or no reality in sin. If sin were real and enduring, like goodness and Truth, it could not be forgiven but would hold its victim forever. When we enter into the understanding of the real and the unreal, a great light dawns on us, and we see what Jesus meant when He said, "The Son of man hath authority on earth to forgive sins."

forgiveness, necessity of—Our first work in any demonstration is to contact God; therefore, we must forgive all men their transgressions. Through the divine law of forgiveness we cleanse our mind so that the Father can forgive us.

form—"The shape and structure of anything" (Webster). All forms are manifestations of ideas. Back of the universe are both the original creative idea and the cosmic rays that form into earthly things.

fornication—Debasement of the spiritual nature, caused by functioning in carnal consciousness.

fornication, abstaining from—Refusing to entertain mortal tendencies and dwelling in spiritual consciousness.

forsaking all for Christ—Giving up everything pertaining to the personal man, so that the Mind of Christ may be perfectly incorporated into consciousness.

fourth dimension—A transcendent realm that Jesus called the "kingdom of the heavens." Here one can discern the trend of spiritual forces and see with the spiritual vision of the Christ Mind.

The fourth dimension (which embraces and encompasses the other three dimensions) is also realization, the doing away with time and space and all conditions. The human mind, with its limited reasoning faculties, is bound by time, space, and conditions and can get no farther into the spiritual than reason will take it, but when we go beyond reason into the realm of realization, then we have attained the consciousness of pure being, the fourth-dimension mind.

frankincense—"A fragrant gum resin" (Webster). Metaphysically, it represents in man the transmutation of the material consciousness into the spiritual.

freedom—The quality or state of being without thought or restraint, bondage, limitation, or repression; having a sense of complete well-being. It is a result of regulating one's life according to Principle, not according to what anyone else may·think or say.

We can never know the full meaning of freedom until we abide in the Christ consciousness. Without prayer and spiritual meditation there can be no concept of spiritual freedom and, therefore, no demonstration of it. It is gained only through spiritual development gained in long hours of communion with God in the silence. Liberation from bondage comes as we seek first the perfect Mind of Christ. "If therefore the Son shall make you free, ye shall be free indeed" (John 8:36).

free will—Man's inherent freedom to act as he determines. There can be no perfect expression without perfect freedom of will. If man determines to act in accord with divine law, he builds harmony, health, happiness, and eternal life, which is heaven.

fruitfulness—The rich consciousness man develops as the result of high realizations of Truth.

fruit of the vine—The "fruit of the vine," which man drinks anew in the Father's kingdom, is the consciousness of spiritual life direct from the Fountainhead. (see Matt. 26:29)

fulfill—"To carry into effect; to realize or manifest completely" (Webster). To fulfill the law of his being, man must proclaim the true word and thought of unity with God.

fulfillment of righteousness—Attained through affirmation of Truth and denial of error. As man dwells "in the secret place of the Most High," "under the shadow of the Almighty" (Psalms 91:1, 2), he will fulfill all righteousness.

G

garden—The spiritual body in which man dwells when he brings forth thoughts after the pattern of original divine ideas. This "garden" is the substance of God.

Garden of Eden—Represents a region of Being in which are provided all primal ideas for the production of the beautiful; the elemental life and intelligence placed at the disposal of man, through which he is to evolve.

Man's body temple is the outer expression of the Garden of Eden. God gave it to man "to dress it and to keep it." (see Gen. 2:15) Man's primary work in the earthly consciousness is to use his creative power to preserve harmony and order in his world and to conserve his powers for divine direction. (see *Eden, Garden of*)

garment—The radiation or aura that surrounds the body.

garment, Jesus' seamless—The indivisible garment that Jesus wore next to His body. It was a thought garment woven without a break of His high realizations of Truth. These realizations of Truth not only infolded Him but firmly interlaced the substance of both His spiritual and body consciousness.

gate, narrow—The spiritual mind, which requires absolute conformity to Truth and measures all things by the gauge of Truth. The way is "straitened" because it requires only Truth to be recognized, and it rules out untruth or evil.

gate, wide—The easy, negative way by which men conform to sense consciousness and the pleasures of the world, with the result that their mind-muscle becomes soft and flabby. When trials come men find that they are not able to cope with them.

gates, twelve—The twelve faculties of mind. Before these faculties become avenues through which we enter into the city of God, they must be purified according to the standards of Spirit.

Gehenna—Represents the cleansing fire of Spirit, which consumes all the dross of sense and materiality. (see *hell*)

generation—Procreation. The law of generation is undoubtedly the mystery of mysteries in human consciousness. Men have probed, with more or less success, all the secrets of nature, but of the origin of life they know comparatively nothing. It is only when the inquiring mind transcends the human and rises into the spiritual realm that light comes.

generic—"Pertaining to, or having the rank of, a genus" (Webster). Family; kind. Adam was generic man, the whole human race epitomized in an individual man idea. "Let the earth put forth grass, herbs yielding seed, *and* fruit-trees bearing fruit after their kind" (Gen. 1:11).

Genesis—Source or origin. The first of the "five books of Moses," giving an account of creation from a metaphysical viewpoint.

genius—One who lets Spirit within him speak out, regardless of how different the utterances may be from those of persons who pose as authorities. He has absolute faith in his spiritual revelations and fearlessly proclaims them. He is a pioneer and a leader. He listens to his own inner voice and has faith in his God-given ability.

ghosts—Thoughts objectified. They are nothing except mind projections.

giants—The Philistines and all the other giants of the Promised Land represent the untrained or undeveloped states of mind in the subconsciousness that Truth is to subdue and to discipline. When they become obedient to the law of Being they will be man's servants, gladly doing his bidding.

gift—"Every good gift and every perfect gift is from above, coming down from the Father of lights" (James

1:17). God's greatest gift to man is the power of thought, through which he can incorporate into his consciousness the Mind of God.

gift, spiritual—The manifestation of Spirit in each of the members of the Christ body according to each man's receptivity; giving to each member a particular work in the redemption of the individual.

gifts, of the Magi—Offerings of love to the Christ; inner resources open to the Christ Mind.

giving, and receiving—It is necessary to give freely if we are to receive freely. The law of receiving includes giving. The knowledge that substance is omnipresent and that man cannot, therefore, impoverish himself by giving (but rather will increase his supply) will enable man to give freely and cheerfully. "Freely ye received, freely give" (Matt. 10:8).

glorify—To magnify with praise; to enhance with spiritual splendor; to adorn. Glorification is the highest spiritual state of consciousness attainable by man.

glory—Realization of divine unity; the blending and merging of man's mind with God-Mind.

goat—Metaphysically, the goat symbolizes resistance and opposition. It is a phase of personality. We resist Spirit on one hand and we resist fellow men on the other. Resistance to the Lord is to be killed out entirely, and resistance to our fellowmen is to be sent into the wilderness (denied a place in consciousness).

God—The almighty One; the Creator; the ruler of the universe; the Infinite; the Eternal. God is not person but Principle. He is the underlying, unchangeable Truth "with whom can be no variation, neither shadow that is cast by turning" (James 1:17). God as principle is absolute good expressed in all creation. When men know God and worship Him "in spirit and truth" (John 4:24), they recognize Him as this great goodness, omnipresent, omniscient, and omnipotent. "Blessed *be* . . . God . . . the

Father of mercies and God of all comfort" (II Cor. 1:3)

God is personal to us when we recognize Him within us as our indwelling life, intelligence, love, and power. There is a difference between a personal God and God personal to us. Since the word *personal* sometimes leads to misunderstanding, it would probably be better to speak of God individualized in man rather than of God personal to man.

When we identify ourselves with Him as our indwelling Father, He seems to us to be personal; however, it is not in a personal sense, but in the universal identification of ourselves with Him that we come into the God consciousness. The personal is limited. The universal, or God consciousness, is unlimited.

God is that from which all love springs. His character is taught in the name *Father,* representing the love, protection, and providing care of God for man, His offspring. He is life and love and wisdom and power and strength and substance.

We do not see God with our physical eyes except as He manifests Himself through His works. His attributes are, therefore, brought into expression by man, who is His son and who is like Him in essence. If we would make of ourselves channels through which He can come forth into expression and manifestation, we must endeavor to raise our thought and feeling to God's level.

God, accessibility of—God is approachable, available, and usable to all who draw nigh unto Him. God is Spirit, the principle of intelligence and life, everywhere present at all times. He is, forever, as accessible as a principle of mathematics or music. "The Father abiding in me" (John 14:10).

God as health—God is absolute wholeness and perfection. Man's recognition of his oneness with this perfect wholeness through Christ brings him into the consciousness of his indwelling life and health. "I in them, and thou in me, that they may be perfected into one" (John 17:23).

God as law—Principle in action.

God as lawgiver—The law of God in action is the Holy Spirit; in that action He appears as having individuality. When prophets and mystics come into conscious mental touch with this executive lawgiver, He uses them as mouthpieces by which He guides and directs His people.

God as life—God as life is made manifest in the living. Life cannot be analyzed by the senses. It is beyond their grasp; hence, it must be cognized by the higher consciousness.

God as mind—The connecting link between God and man. God-Mind embraces all knowledge, wisdom, and understanding and is the source of every manifestation of true knowledge and intelligence. God as principle cannot be comprehended by any of the senses. But the mind of man is limitless, and through it he may come into touch with Divine Mind. The one Mind is a unit and cannot be divided. The individual mind is a state of consciousness in the one Mind.

God as principle—The unchangeable life, love, substance, and intelligence of Being. Principle does not occupy space; neither has it any limitations of time or matter, but it eternally exists as the one underlying cause out of which come forth all true ideas.

God as Spirit—God is Spirit, and Spirit is located and appears wherever it is recognized by an intelligent entity. It thus follows that whoever gives his attention to Spirit and seals his identification with it by His word, starts a flow of Spirit life and all the attributes of Spirit in and through his consciousness. To the extent that man practices identifying himself with the one and only source of existence, he becomes Spirit, until finally the union attains a perfection in which he can say with Jesus, "I and the Father are one" (John 10:30).

God as substance—This does not mean matter, because matter is formed while God is the formless. The
substance that God is lies back of all matter and all forms.
It is that which is the basis of all form yet enters not into
any form as finality. It cannot be seen, tasted, or touched.
Yet it is the only enduring substance in the universe.

God as Truth—The eternal verity of the universe and
man.

God, centered in—To have the attention focused on
spiritual ideas and ideals.

God, creative process of—Christianity describes God
as Spirit, creating by a process comparable to the mental
processes, with which we are all familiar. First, mind, then
the idea (word) in mind of what the act shall be, then
the act itself. God planned man and the universe, and
through the expression of His word projected them into
creation, as ideal principles and imminent energies acting
behind and within all visibility. The creative processes
of Divine Mind are continuously operative; creation is
going on all the time, but the over-all plan, the design
in Divine Mind, is finished.

God's creations are always spiritual. This includes
spiritual man (God-man) through whom all things, including personal man (Adam man) are brought into
manifestation. Spiritual man is the acme or pinnacle of
God's creation—the image and likeness of God. "Thou
art my beloved Son, in thee I am well pleased" (Mark 1:
11).

God, demonstrating—To demonstrate God means to
make His Spirit manifest in one's life.

God immanent—This refers to the all-pervading and
indwelling presence of God, the life and intelligence per-
meating the universe. Jesus lovingly revealed that the Father is within man, forever resident in the invisible side
of man's nature. Paul also set forth this truth when he

wrote of "one God and Father of all, who is over all, and through all, and in all" (Eph. 4:6).

God, jealous—God is not jealous as men count jealousy, but He is jealous of principle, from which no lapses are tolerated. Man's failure to observe divine law causes it to react on him.

God-man—The man that God created in His image and likeness, and present within all men.

God manifest—God manifest is really greater than God principle; the man who has demonstrated the God character is greater than the untried man. Jesus proclaimed, "I and the Father are one" (John 10:30). He had all the possibilities of Principle and, in addition, He demonstrated a large degree of its possibilities. In this respect, Jesus is the great Way-Shower and helper for all men.

God presence, unity with—To make oneself conscious of the presence of God, one must consistently affirm oneness with this presence. Say: *"I have faith in God; I have faith in Spirit; I have faith in things invisible. I am one with God."*

God, reconciliation with—To be reconciled with God means to be willing that His will be done; that is, that limitations, personality, ignorance shall give way so that the perfection and righteousness of Divine Mind may be expressed. Reconciliation takes place by man's surrender of an adverse will and an acceptance of that "mind . . . which was also in Christ Jesus" (Phil. 2:5).

God, responsibility to—Truth is implanted in us by divine intelligence. To the degree that we awaken to the consciousness of the inherent wisdom, to this degree are we responsible to the Father and required to render unto Him the fruitage of our wisdom. Each of us unfolds according to understanding and realization. Whether our understanding is little or great, we must demonstrate the Truth we know. If our understanding is much, much is required of us.

"God said"—The same as "Mind thought," by which all things were brought forth. (see 1st chapter of Genesis)

God transcendent—This suggests God as above and beyond His creation. That God is remote from the practical affairs of man or from man's own experience is a false belief. God (perfection) is not out of reach of His offspring; neither is He something beyond and above man. Tennyson tells us that "closer is He than breathing, and nearer than hands and feet."

God, will of—God's will is always perfection and all good for all His children; perfect health in mind and body; abundance of every good thing including joy, peace, wisdom, and eternal life. He does not will suffering or imperfection in any form.

The belief that God wills both good and evil is false; the truth is that God is all good and only good can come to man from Him. If man experiences error and inharmony, he brings them upon himself by his failure to harmonize his thoughts, words, and acts with the Lord, or divine law.

God's name—God's name represents wholeness. It is holy, perfect. God is everywhere present. When we think of God as being anything less than that which is perfect and whole, we are taking His name in vain. "Thou shalt not take the name of Jehovah thy God in vain" (Exod. 20:7).

gold—Metaphysically, gold represents spiritual gifts; the riches of Spirit. The gold that the Wise Men brought to the Christ child was a consciousness of the omnipresent richness of substance. To follow Jesus in the demonstration of prosperity, we must charge our mind with wise and rich ideas.

golden candlesticks—Receptacles of spiritual light.

golden scepter—A rod; symbol of wisdom held out when the king (the will) is willing to listen to reason.

Golgotha—"The place of a skull" (Matt. 27:33). The skull is the place where the intellect is crossed out, so that Spirit may win eternal ascendancy. Jesus (the intellectual) was crucified at "The place of a skull," so that Christ (Truth) might become all in all.

good, the—The Absolute; the incomparable; that which is godly in its character. God is omnipresent All-Good. "Why callest thou me good? none is good save one, *even* God" (Mark 10:18).

good and evil states of consciousness—Good and evil states of consciousness form the heavens and the hells of the race. We go in mind to heaven or hell every time we mentally project thoughts that "chord" with that particular state. When we establish an enduring consciousness of good, evil disappears as darkness before light.

goodness, reward of—There is always a saving grace in divine goodness; and if we have ever done a kind act, it has been preserved in the careful records of memory and will come forth when we most need it.

gospel—An Anglo-Saxon word derived from *God* (good) and *spell* (story, tidings). It is now universally identified with Jesus' mission and the doctrine that has grown out of it—that system of religious beliefs centered about the teachings of Jesus.

The gospel of Jesus is that every man can become God incarnate. It is not alone a gospel of right living, but also shows the way into dominion and power equal to and surpassing that of Jesus of Nazareth. "He that believeth on me, the works that I do shall he do also; and greater *works* than these shall he do; because I go unto the Father" (John 14:12).

grace—Good will; favor; disposition to show mercy; aid from God in the process of regeneration. "By grace have ye been saved" (Eph. 2:5).

"Grace and truth came through Jesus Christ" (John 1:17); that is, the real saving, redeeming, transforming power came to man through the work that Jesus did in establishing for the race a new and higher consciousness in the earth. We can enter into this consciousness by faith in Him and by means of the inner spirit of the law that He taught and practiced.

gratitude—Gratitude and thanksgiving are both necessary in demonstrating prosperity through divine law. Be grateful to God and thankful to the friends whom He uses to supply you.

All metaphysicians have found by experience that being thankful for what they have increases the inflow. Gratitude is a great mind magnet, and when it is expressed from the spiritual standpoint it is powerfully augmented. The saying of grace at the table has its origin in this idea of the power of increase through giving thanks.

graven image—Idol. We set up a graven image when we image God as a material form or location in substance. (see *image*)

gravitation—The love force in nature; the power of attraction among physical bodies.

greatest in God's kingdom—When Jesus washed the feet of His apostles He brought home to His followers that he who willingly performs lowly, humble service for others, with no thought of personal distinction, is greatest in God's kingdom.

greed, freedom from—A result of the habit of tithing, which establishes a consciousness of giving and keeps one's mental channel free from material selfishness.

Greek—Metaphysically, a term for intellectual reasoning. In Acts 11:20-24, the truth regarding the new teaching of Jesus is beginning to reach the old reasoning of the intellect, and the wall of old ideas is being broken down.

ground, holy—Substance in its spiritual wholeness, or the idea of substance in Divine Mind. When we realize this idea we let go of all limitation and are conscious only of the Absolute.

growth—Increase by assimilation of new substance; multiplication. We grow by incorporating spiritual substance into our consciousness. The law of growth is in beholding. When we behold the body as anything other than its divine idea, we hold it there (in error, sin, discord). To behold ourselves free from these keeps us manifesting freedom.

growth, spiritual—The increase of God in man. All growth is first in mind and depends on the standards we are holding in mind. A high spiritual standard has lifting power. All growth and unfoldment are based on the law. What we earnestly desire and persistently affirm will be ours if we "faint not" (Gal. 6:9).

guidance, spiritual—The impressions that come from the Spirit of truth within man.

H

hades—A Greek word, often translated *hell*. It is supposed to refer to the unseen world, or the abode of the dead. In reality, however, the word has reference to the grave or the "pit." Hades refers to the outer darkness, the realm of sense, in contrast to the inner or luminously spiritual.

hallow the name of God—To realize that His name means wholeness and perfection for us.

halo—The artists of old always painted saints with an emanation or circle of light around the head, which custom contained a grain of truth. It is from the I AM center in the crown of the head that we draw all new inspiration, all new ideas. When they contact man's consciousness these new inspirations, new ideas, break forth as a soft golden light (pure wisdom) that surrounds the head. This is known to spiritually quickened men as the halo. (see *aura*)

hand—Represents executive ability; the doing of things; outer or manual power.

hardening—Refusing to accept guidance of Spirit. Willful ignorance of the God principle in man's own being, or disobedience to the indwelling Christ.

harmony, divine—Perfect accord with the goodness, the beauty, and the righteousness of omnipresent Spirit. Everything is governed by fixed law, and harmony is its expression. This is illustrated by the living body, which is a sensitive instrument, responsive to the touch of the Master, I AM.

harmony, divine, how lost—When the will is centered in the external and loses sight of the ideal, it breaks the connection between Spirit and manifestation, and thus man loses the harmony that is his under divine law.

harmony, divine, how restored—Through a knowledge of the Truth of Being man is restored to divine harmony. He must know the Truth about himself and conform to it in all his thinking, and not be misled by appearances.

hate—Extreme antipathy, intense aversion, lingering antagonism. Dislike is a mild form of hate. Both hatred and dislike are antichrist, and have no place in the superconsciousness.

hate, bodily effects of—Hate burns out the vital spark in the glands, much as an excessively high current burns out a fuse in your house lighting system. Then the light goes out and death of the body sets in.

hate, remedy for—Love, peace, and harmony are the only remedies that count. "God is love" (I John 4:8), and to live in God-Mind, man must cultivate love until it becomes the keynote of his life.

head—The center from which the mind expresses various thoughts and ideas.

heal—"To make hale, sound, or whole" (Webster). To bring forth the perfect Christ man that exists within each of us.

healer—One who heals the sins of man, and restores him to his original, sinless state. The healer is the focal center of faith; through him faith reaches the patient, directly or by means of someone very much interested in him.

healer, natural—One who has a great compassion and yearning to help humanity out of its errors and suffering. When one enters this state of consciousness a healing virtue pours out that changes all discord to harmony.

healing—"Restoring to original purity or integrity" (Webster). The first step in all spiritual healing is to believe, and the next step is openness and receptivity to the stream of healing life. Through the exercise of faith and our words, our spiritual quality is fused into unity with the power of Christ and the work is marvelously accomplished.

All healing is based on mental cleansing. When the mind is free from error thoughts, harmony in the body ensues. Permanent healing is never accomplished until the mental cause of the disease, the error thought, is removed. Jesus was a true healer, and when He cast out the error that caused the condition, He said, "Sin no more, lest a worse thing befall thee" (John 5:14). The "thing" was caused by sin. Thus the true way to heal is to find the mental cause and destroy it forever.

healing, absent—Healing of an individual by a person who is not in the physical presence of the one being healed.

healing and will power—Through the use of the will, it is possible to bring about an appearance of health. This is not spiritual healing; it is a species of mind dominance.

healing, medical and spiritual—Permanent healing is never gained through medication or drug curing. Spiritual healing restores to perpetual health because it erases the error thought and cleanses the mind. "Though your sins be as scarlet, they shall be as white as snow" (Isa. 1:18).

healing name—Any declaration man may make, in which the name *Jesus Christ* is used reverently, will contact the spiritual ether where the Christ I AM lives and will open the mind and body to the inflow of spiritual healing power. Affirm: *Through Jesus Christ, vitalizing energy floods my whole being, and I am healed.*

healing, psychical—Healing on the mental plane.

healing virtue—The restoring power of Being. "For power came forth from him, and healed *them* all" (Luke 6:19).

healing word—The healing word is not a special creation to meet an emergency. The word goes forth and establishes that which is. It does not heal anything—in its perfection there is nothing to heal. Its office is to behold the perfection of Being.

health—A state of being sound or whole in mind and body. Oneness with the Christ Mind assures perfect health. Health is the normal condition of man, a condition true to the Truth of his being. Health is from within and does not have to be manufactured in the without. It is the very essence of Being, universal and enduring.

That which seems to be sickness does not exist in Truth. When man becomes so much at one with God-Mind that he abides in the consciousness of health, he enters the eternal peace in which he knows that "it is finished" (John 19:30). To know God as health one must take up the study of the healthy mind and make it and not physical appearance the basis of every calculation.

health and the word—Experiences, innumerable times repeated, prove the power of words to bring health. Health is potential in the real of your being. Health can always be demonstrated through the power of the spoken word.

hearing—Ability to look deeper than words and catch

the inner meaning. "He that hath ears, let him hear" (Matt. 13:9). In many places the Bible indicates that the ear referred to is not the physical organ but the listening mind.

The "ear" that conceives and really hears is the auditory center in the brain. It is here that the mind grasps and analyzes the sound vibrations.

heart—The heart is love, the affectional consciousness in man. It is the faculty through which man receives love from Being. The heart, however, is but the visible expression of an invisible center of consciousness. It is the center from which the divine substance is poured forth. Everyone uses his heart center when he sends forth a loving thought.

As used in Scripture, the word *heart* represents the subconscious mind. "Out of the abundance of the heart his mouth speaketh" (Luke 6:45).

heart, good and evil—The heart of the unregenerate man is both good and evil, but the evil is without foundation in Being, and has no sustaining power outside man's belief in its reality. When the heart is purged of all thoughts adverse to good, man consciously contacts the underlying God substance.

heaven—The Christ consciousness; the realm of Divine Mind; a state of consciousness in harmony with the thoughts of God. Heaven is everywhere present. It is the orderly, lawful adjustment of God's kingdom in man's mind, body, and affairs.

Jesus, of all those claiming intimate acquaintance with spiritual things, gave heaven definite location. "The kingdom of God is within you" (Luke 17:21). Heaven is within every one of us; a place, a conscious sphere of mind, having all the attraction described or imagined as belonging to heaven. But this kingdom within is not material, it is spiritual.

heaven and earth—Two states of mind, the ideal and the manifestation. According to Revelation 21:1 we are to have new ideals with manifestations in the earth to correspond.

God visioned two planes of consciousness, the heaven and the earth, or more properly, "the heavens and the earth." One is the realm of pure ideas; the other, of thought forms. Heaven is the orderly realization of divine ideas. Earth is the manifestation of these ideas.

heaven, firmament of—The consciousness of Truth that has been formulated and established.

heaven, restoration to—Faith in Spirit and the ultimate dominance of the good in all men will finally restore man to the heavenly consciousness from which he descended.

heifer—The heifer, she-goat, ram, turtledove, and young pigeon that Abram was instructed to take (Gen. 15:9) represent beliefs on the sense plane that must be sacrificed. The thought of physical strength must be given up, and its spiritual source must be realized. The human must be given up in order that the divine will may prevail. All subconscious resistance to the working of the divine law must be denied away.

hell—Symbolized in the Bible as Gehenna, Ge Hinnom, the Valley of Hinnom—a place outside Jerusalem where the city's refuse was burned. It symbolizes that purifying fire which consumes the dross of man's character.

Metaphysically, hell represents a corrective state of mind. When error has reached its limit, the retroactive law asserts itself, and judgment, being part of that law, brings the penalty, called hell, upon the transgressor. This penalty is not punishment, but discipline. If the transgressor is repentant and obedient, he is forgiven. (see *fire, hades*)

hell of fire—The "hell of fire" spoken of in Scripture is the purifying fire or power of the Spirit. Its purpose is the cleansing and purification of man.

heredity, flesh—The belief that man has his being from man. The law is that like begets like, and this law is set into operation in a way adverse to Truth when man holds himself as the offspring of mortal man. It is overcome by the Truth that God is Father, that man's real source is God, and that his inheritance is the perfection and wholeness of God. When this Truth is perceived we begin to understand and take on the characteristics of our divine Father. If we believe that God is our Father, and acknowledge Him, He will acknowledge us.

"hid with Christ in God"—The lifting up of the Christ in man in order that his physical and mental nature may be drawn into the universal perfection. Man dies to the old life of sense and lives under a new commandment. "For ye died, and your life is hid with Christ in God" (Col. 3:3).

hireling—The hireling state of mind is that in which one is constantly looking for rewards. This cultivates selfishness, which is the foundation of fear.

hoarding—Gathering things together in the external. This is a vain effort to avert an imagined shortage in the future. "Lay not up for yourselves treasures upon the earth, where moth and rust consume . . . but lay up for yourselves treasures in heaven, where neither moth nor rust doth consume" (Matt. 6:19, 20).

hold all persons in Truth—Never to think evil of anyone, no matter how much error he may seem to express, but to see all as they really are in Spirit: perfect, harmonious, joyous, and prosperous.

hold a thought—To search out and absorb to one's consciousness, through the process of meditation and prayer, the Truth contained in spiritual words. To repeat some statement of Truth in the silence and meditate on it until it becomes a living word in the consciousness, illuminating and upbuilding mind and body.

holding a mental picture—This is a work that lies deeper than the outer man discerns. The subconscious mind must enter into the process and desire intensely the good that is to be demonstrated. This deep desire keeps in mind an image of that which is to be brought into manifestation.

holding to Principle—Standing steadfast by a statement of Truth in the face of seeming error; insisting on the divine accuracy of one's faith. Demonstration will follow.

holy—"Spiritually whole; of unimpaired innocence" (Webster). Holiness is wholeness in Spirit, mind, and body. In this state of consciousness man is aware of the all-pervading glory of God.

Holy Communion—To establish our acceptance of the Christ we celebrate Holy Communion within our mind and heart. "And as they were eating, Jesus took bread, and blessed, and brake it; and he gave to the disciples, and said, Take, eat; this is my body. And he took a cup, and gave thanks, and gave to them, saying, Drink ye all of it; for this is my blood of the covenant . . . I shall not drink henceforth of this fruit of the vine, until that day when I drink it new with you in my Father's kingdom" (Matt. 26:26-29).

The bread used in the churches typifies substance, which we consider the Lord's body, a body of spiritual ideas. The wine used symbolizes His blood, life, or the circulation of divine ideas in our consciousness that will purify our mind and heart and renew our strength, freeing us from all corruption, sin, and evil, and bringing forth in us the abundant unlimited life of God. Through the appropriation and assimilation of substance and life in consciousness, we blend our mind with the Father-Mind, or universal Mind of God, and there is a harmonizing of every fiber of the body with Christ. As our mind and heart are cleansed of untrue thoughts and beliefs, our body will take on the life and light of divinity. Eventually, the body will become living light, as was shown in the transfiguration of Jesus.

Holy Ghost—(see *Holy Spirit*)

holy ground—(see *ground, holy*)

holy, holy, holy—The word of Truth; the statement of wholeness of the whole body; a spiritual perception of the all-pervading glory of divine perfection.

holy of holies—The most sacred inner realm of consciousness wherein man comes into awareness of the presence of Spirit.

Holy Spirit—The activity of God in a universal sense. The moving force in the universe taken as a whole. The Spirit is the infinite "breath" of God, the life essence of Being. "And when he had said this, he breathed on them, and saith unto them, Receive ye the Holy Spirit" (John 20:22).

Holy Spirit is the love of Jehovah taking care of the human family. The Holy Spirit is in the world today with great power and wisdom, ready to be poured upon all who look to it for guidance. Its mission is to bring all men into communion with God; to guide men in order that they will not mistake the way into the light.

The Holy Spirit is third in the Trinity, which in theology is designated: Father, Son, and Holy Spirit. In metaphysics we approach the Trinity and more readily realize its meaning through the terms mind, idea, and expression. To be "filled with the Holy Spirit" is to realize the activities of Spirit in individual consciousness. The quickening of a man by the Holy Spirit is peculiar to each individual and must be experienced to be understood.

The Holy Spirit is authority on the gospel of Jesus. It is the only authority that Jesus ever recognized, and whoever attempts to set forth His gospel from any other standpoint is in the letter and not the spirit. No man can know what Jesus' doctrine is except he gets it direct from the one and only custodian. It is not to come secondhand, but each for himself must receive it from the Holy Spirit, which is sent by the Father in the name of the Son.

Holy Spirit, sin against—Resistance to Spirit. So

long as it continues, it shuts out the forgiving love of God.

Holy Spirit and the Word—The Word is man's I AM identity. The Holy Spirit is the outpouring or activity of the living Word. The activity produces the light of Spirit, the Truth of God, the personality of Being.

holy temple—The redeemed spiritual body.

honesty—The divine law in action, which reveals that man must give an equivalent (equal value) for everything that he gets. "That we may lead a quiet and peaceable life in all godliness and honesty" (I Tim. 2:2, Scofield).

hope (and faith)—Hope is the expectation of good in the future. It is a quality (good as far as it goes) of sense mind because it is subject to time. Faith is the certain knowledge that our good is ours right now. It is of God; it goes beyond time and space.

horns, ram's—Adverse conditions. The blowing of the ram's horn represents the denial of adverse conditions and the affirmation of the power of Spirit.

horses, four—(see 6th chapter of Revelation.) The four horses and their riders are, first, "a white horse," representing the power of the Christ; second, "a red horse [war]: and to him that sat thereon it was given to take peace from the earth"; third, "a black horse" [commercialism]: "A measure of wheat for a shilling, and three measures of barley for a shilling"; and fourth, "a pale horse: and he that sat upon him, his name was Death."

Prodigious preparation for war by nations, incited by the greed for gain, will lead them to "let slip the dogs of war" unless the rider of the white horse comes forth "conquering, and to conquer."

hosannas—Represent the joyful obedience and homage that all the thoughts in one's consciousness give when an error state of mind is overcome.

house—The house that God builds and dwells in is man's body. "Know ye not that your body is a temple [house] of the Holy Spirit?" (I Cor. 6:19). The body temple. "For we are a temple of the living God" (II Cor. 6:16).

humanity—The garden of God, of which the soil is the omnipresent thought substance.

humility—"Freedom from pride and arrogance" (Webster). Recognition that the personal man by himself is ineffectual. "I can of myself do nothing" (John 5:30). "The Father abiding in me doeth his works" (John 14:10).

True humility is needed very much in the Christ-centered individual. The true Christian is humble. He knows the nothingness of the lesser self in man and the allness of Christ.

hypocrite—In classic Greek, the word meant an actor in a theater; so the word came to mean anyone who pretends to be one thing while really he is something far different.

Appearing to be lovingly thoughtful for others, while thinking only of self and reputation, is to deserve only the reward of a hypocrite. No wise man would seek the reward of empty applause, which might satisfy the boastful giver. A modest man asks the approval of Spirit only. (see Matt. 6:1-18)

I

I AM—Spiritual identity; the real or Christ Mind, of each individual. The I AM Being. God is I AM, and man, His offspring, is also I AM. I AM is the indwelling Lord of life, love, wisdom, and all the ideas eternally in Divine Mind.

The I AM is the metaphysical name of the spiritual self, as distinguished from the human self. One is governed by Spirit, the other by personal will. Christ and Jehovah are the scriptural names for spiritual I AM. Jesus called it the Father. I AM is eternal, without beginning or ending: the true spiritual man whom God made in His image and likeness.

The I AM has its being in heaven; its home is in the realm of God ideals. It is the center around which all the thoughts of man revolve. The narrow concept of the personal I AM should be led out into the consciousness of the great and only I AM. Man identifies himself with that to which he attaches his I AM, and whatever he identifies himself with, that he manifests. Hitch your I AM to the star of Christ, and infinite joy will follow as night the day.

I AM identity—As the will of God, man represents I AM identity. Individual consciousness is like an eddy in the ocean—all the elements that are found in the ocean are also found in the eddy, and every eddy may, in due course, receive and give forth all that is in the ocean. This is individual consciousness, freedom to act without dictation of any kind, selfhood without consciousness of cause, the power to make or break without limitation.

I AM, used adversely—Man seeking happiness through sense pleasure. This is sin (missing the mark), and the wages are pain, sickness, poverty, and death. Think I AM in harmony with God-Mind, and health, wealth, and harmony will be yours.

"I am the light of the world"—(John 8:12). Refers to Christ as the expresser of Truth in all its aspects.

idea—Original, primary, or unlimited thought of Being; in God-Mind the eternal Word or Logos.

The first-born of everything in the universe is an idea in Divine Mind. The divine idea of the universal creation is called in Scripture Christ, "who is the image of the invisible God, the first born of all creation" (Col. 1:15). Everything is first an idea in mind, and this law holds good, not only in the creations of God, but in the forms made by man as well. The table upon which you write was first an idea in the mind of the maker. All creation is summed up or concentrated in man. Everything found in the universe is found in his constitution. "In him dwelleth all the fulness of the Godhead bodily" (Col. 2:9).

idea, Christ—The one complete idea of perfect man in Divine Mind. Jesus is the name that represents an individual expression of the Christ idea. Jesus Christ is the name often applied to the man of Galilee who demonstrated perfection. Christ Jesus is the idea that is being expressed by men as a result of their faith in and understanding of Truth. In this idea are involved all the potentialities of that which is to be evolved through man. The idea itself becomes the evolving power through which it makes its inherencies manifest.

Christ ideas are the most heavily charged with Spirit. Every expressed idea of the Christ Mind is powerful in raising consciousness. Jesus could well say, "I, if I be lifted up from the earth, will draw all men unto myself" (John 12:32).

ideas are catching—We are all heavily charged with ideas, and when these ideas are released they spring forth and pass from mind to mind, being "recorded" as they fly; when they are expressed the whole race is lifted up—if the idea is charged with the uplifting Spirit.

ideas, relation of, to the mind—As the son is to the father, so is the idea to the mind. Mind is one with its ideas, so the Father (God-Mind) is one with its offspring, the idea, the Son. Mind is coexistent with its ideas, and there is continual interaction and communion.

ideal—A mental pattern of perfection.

ideal, divine—The Christ man; the divine idea of man.

ideal of Spirit—The ideals in the Mind of Being that produce the perfect creation.

ideal unfoldment—When the illumined intellect wholly co-operates with Spirit there is a merging and blending of these powers until the intellect ceases to be mere intellect and is lost in Spirit.

idealism, divine—God's standard of perfection.

idol—In scriptural language, a false god. Even as Jesus was tempted by Satan, we are often tempted to worship the false gods of greed, covetousness, jealousy, retaliation, and other forms of negation.

ignorance, how dissolved—Ignorance (lack of knowledge) that results from association with ignorant minds can be dissolved by using the Word.

ills, cause of—Anger, jealousy, fear, hate, lust often cause ills of the body. These result from our failure to adjust our mind to Divine Mind. When the sinning state of mind is forgiven and the heavenly state of mind established, man is restored to his primal and natural wholeness. "The Son of man hath authority on earth to forgive sins" (Luke 5:24). This is wholly a mind process. All wrong and right conditions of man result from his thinking. "As he thinketh within himself, so is he" (Prov. 23:7).

illumination—The light of Christ; spiritual understanding; intuitive knowing. Spiritual illumination is a state of consciousness resulting from Holy Spirit baptism. It is good to affirm: *"Christ radiance lights my mind, and my whole being is illumined with Truth."*

illumined consciousness—A mind purified by the light of Truth.

illumined thoughts—Thoughts quickened through their conscious relationship to Spirit.

illusion—(see *ghosts*)

image—"A mental representation of anything not actually present to the senses" (Webster). Everything that is manifested was first a mental picture and was brought into expression by the forming power of the imagination. Man accumulates a mass of ideas about substance and life, and with his imagination he molds them into shape. Each one of us must not only see the image of our desires as a theory, but we must also form it into a living, breathing thing through every motive and act.

Man gets the ideal images necessary to express his perfect organism from the one perfect Mind. The perfect body will be demonstrated through his beholding the perfect, eternal, living, glorified Christ body.

image, graven—(Exod. 20:4). Graven images of God are made by mental pictures. The thought of God as a great king in a place called heaven makes just such a material image in our thought realm, and we grow to believe in and worship such an imaginary being, instead of the true God, who is Spirit.

imagination—The faculty of mind that images and forms; the power to shape and form thought. The imaging faculty presides at the nerve center between the eyes. Through this faculty the formless takes form.

With our imagination we lay hold of ideas and clothe them with substance. The body is the product of the mind. What man pictures or imagines in his mind will eventually appear in his body. In the communication of God with man, the imaging power of the mind plays an important part. It receives divine ideas and reflects their character to the consciousness. According to Scripture this is the opening of the heavens and the seeing the "angels of God ascending and descending upon the Son of man" (John 1:51).

immaculate conception—(Luke 1:26-35). The coming into activity of the Christ in us is the result of an exalted idea sown in the mind. Therefore Mary, the soul, becomes devout and expectant and believes in the so-called miraculous as a possibility. Mary expected the birth of the Messiah as the Holy Spirit had promised. She was overshadowed by that high idea, and it formed in her mind the seed that quickened into the cell. In due season there were aggregations of cells strong enough in their activity, and what is called the birth of Jesus took place.

Metaphysically interpreted, Mary, the virgin mother, represents a pure state of mind that ponders spiritual

things and believes in revelations from angels and messengers from God.

Mary was "found with child of the Holy Spirit," which
refers to the miraculous conception by which the Virgin
Mary is held to have conceived without original sin.
Joseph, not fully understanding the prophecy, "was
minded to put her away privily," which refers to the fact
that in the first stages of the birth of Christ in us we do
not understand the process, and sometimes are moved to
put it away from us.

immanent—Indwelling, abiding in, remaining or operating within. God is immanent in all creation including
man. "One God and father of all, who is over all, and
through all, and in all" (Eph. 4:6).

Immanuel (or Emmanuel)—A Hebrew word meaning
"God with us." The consciousness that God is with us and
we are one with Him. The understanding of how "the
Word became flesh" (John 1:14).

immortal—Not subject to death; that which has everlasting existence; incorruptible.

impulse—Metaphysically, a movement of mind that
urges man on to spiritual achievement. That which urges
man to go forward. Thought activity that arises in the
inner, or spiritual mind.

impurity, how eliminated—The consciousness of
personal impurity is taken away through the realization
of divine purity in thoughts and words.

incarnate Word of God—The word of God made
flesh. Spiritual man, Christ, is the incarnate Word of God.

incense—A symbol of prayer. There must be a constant going forth of the word of the Spirit, proclaiming
Truth. This spiritual essence should radiate from center
to circumference, and permeate the whole consciousness.

The symbology of the burning of incense (Luke 1:9) is
transmutation. The finer essences of the body are transmuted to what may be termed the fourth or radiant di-

mension, and a firm foundation laid for an organism of permanent character. Paul calls it the "celestial" body (I Cor. 15:40). This process of transmutation takes place whenever the I AM makes union in the body with the Lord, or higher self.

incorporate—To unite with or introduce into a body. We incorporate spiritual substance into our body through prayer.

individuality—The true self; that which is undivided from God; our spiritual identity; the God part of us. That which characterizes one as a distinct entity or particular manifestation of divine Principle. Individuality is eternal; it can never be destroyed. (see *personality*)

infinite—That which embraces all. The totality of Being including all knowledge, all space, all life; the complete all. That which was from the beginning, is now, and ever shall be. Without end or limitation. It is that which is boundless, immeasurable, inexhaustible. God is infinite and eternal.

influence—"Emanation or effusion, especially of a spiritual or moral force" (Webster). One's mental attitude, thoughts, and words are the creative or destructive influences in one's world. Do not say: *"I am sick," "I am poor," "I am unhappy."* Say: *"I am well," "I am at peace," "I am wealthy."*

inheritance—"A possession or blessing" (Webster). Man's inheritance from God is divine ideas. These ideas find expression, and the expression forms what man calls his good. Back of the expression is the idea.

iniquities—The mental habits that shut God out of the consciousness.

injustice—"Violation of another's rights; wrong" (Webster). The belief in injustice may be overcome by understanding the divine law of justice and fixing faith firmly in it. The remedy for all that appears unjust is denial of condemnation of others or self. Thus the healing and forgiving law of Christ is allowed to function. Say: *"I deny all condemnation, judgment, and criticism of myself and all others."*

inn—(Luke 10:34). One's pure thought; the price of the care received there is paid through overcoming.

inner chamber—(Matt. 6:6). The place within where we consciously meet God. It is also called the "secret place of the Most High" (Psalms 91:1), and the "Holy of holies" (Heb. 9:3). Jesus names it "the Father in me" (John 14:11), and "the kingdom of God . . . within you" (Luke 17:21).

insanity—An unbalanced condition of the faculties of mind. The remedy is to know and realize that the unclouded Christ Mind dominates all one's thinking, and that there is perfect balance and control in both mind and body.

inspiration—Inbreathing of Spirit. The breath of God infused into man, endowing him with super light and life. "He breathed on them, and saith unto them, Receive ye the Holy Spirit" (John 20:22).

inspiration, original—The writings of the Hebrew prophets are good examples of original inspiration, which is divine wisdom.

inspiration, spiritual—An inflow of divine ideas; activity of a spiritual character; understanding that comes from God.

instinct—"The native or hereditary factor in behavior" (Webster). It is akin to intuition. Man instinctively trusts in a higher power.

integration—When all the desire of the mind and heart is to express God, man is made whole, unified, integrated. "Blessed are your eyes, for they see; and your ears, for they hear" (Matt. 13:16). Man is spiritually integrated when he experiences unity of mind and body through the Christ consciousness.

integrity, spiritual—That quality of the consciousness

which makes one unswerving in his conformity to the divine standard.

intellect—"The power or faculty of knowing" (Webster). Intellect is not wise. Wisdom is not its office. Intellect is the executive officer of wisdom, and can do right only when faithfully carrying out the instruction of its principal. Intellect follows the letter of the law.

It is hard for the intellect to realize the spiritual "I AM THAT I AM" (Exod. 3:14). The intellect always argues back and forth, endeavoring to prove that it is the highest authority. Jesus condemned the sins of the intellect, of which self-righteousness is the greatest, as worse than moral sins. People who live wholly in the intellect deny that man can know anything about God, because they do not have quickened faith.

intellectualism—Knowledge as independent of feeling. Literal knowledge without consideration of the Spirit. The devotee of intellectualism is often impractical and unsuccessful; he has accumulated more knowledge than he has wisdom and power to apply.

intelligence—The expression of man's powers and capacities through the avenue of the limited mental attitude termed the intellect. When the same avenue loses its boundaries and catches sight of the great sea of infinite understanding, which is always open to it, it takes on that phase of knowing more properly termed wisdom.

intelligence, divine—Intelligence that accords with or comes from Divine Mind. The next great proclamation of scientific minds will be that one directive intelligence is an essential cause of the harmonious universe.

intemperance—"Immoderate indulgence of appetites or passions" (Webster). Men need and desire the stimulant of Spirit, but not being in spiritual understanding they do not know what it is they crave and they seek satisfaction in material things.

intuition—The natural knowing capacity. Inner knowing; the immediate apprehension of spiritual Truth without resort to intellectual means. The wisdom of the heart. It is very much surer in guidance than the head. When one trusts Spirit and looks to it for understanding, a certain confidence in the invisible good develops. This faith awakens the so-called sixth sense, intuition, or divine knowing. Through the power of intuition, man has direct access to all knowledge and the wisdom of God.

invisible, the—Reality that cannot be seen, touched, or comprehended by any of the outer senses. In this realm a great and mighty work is being accomplished.

invocation—The calling forth of the presence of Spirit through the power of the Word.

involution (and evolution)—Involution (infolding) always precedes evolution (unfolding). That which is involved in mind evolves through matter. (see *evolution*)

J

jealousy—A form of mental bias that blinds the judgment and causes one to act without weighing the consequences. The remedy is a dismissal of the negative thoughts that cause one to be jealous, followed by a fuller trust in the great all-adjusting power of God.

Jehovah—The I AM, the spiritual man, the image and likeness of Elohim God. In the King James Version of the Bible the Hebrew "Jehovah" has been translated "Lord." Lord means an external ruler. Bible students say that Jehovah means the self-existent One, the I AM. Then instead of reading "Lord" we should read I AM. It makes a great difference whether we think of I AM, self-existence within, or "Lord," master without. All Scripture shows that Jehovah means just what God told Moses it meant: I AM. "This is my name for ever, and this is my memorial unto all generations" (Exod. 3:15).

Jehovah, anger of—The anger and wrath of Jehovah are symbolical of the divine law in man in its often strenuous work of revealing and erasing error from the consciousness.

Jehovah God—The most inclusive name for Being. Jehovah represents the individual I AM and God (Elohim) the Universal Principle.

Jerusalem—"Habitation of peace." The spiritual center in consciousness. In man it is the abiding consciousness of spiritual peace. When we go deep into the silent recesses of our beings, we realize a stillness and sweetness beyond expression. A great peace is there—the "peace of God, which passeth all understanding" (Phil. 4:7). This is the point in consciousness where the Spiritual energy of life is strong enough to vitalize adjacent body substance. The substance is physically a nerve center just back of the stomach; spiritually it is the realization of the unfailing substance of Divine Mind.

Jerusalem, feast in—Metaphysically, a receptive state of mind toward all spiritual good.

Jerusalem, new—Spiritual consciousness. It is founded on the twelve fundamental ideas in Divine Mind, each represented by one of the precious stones. (Revelation 21: 19, 20) It is also represented by an association of all people in peace, based on spiritual understanding, purity, and a willingness to be united with Christ.

Jesus—The Man of Nazareth, son of Mary; the Saviour of mankind according to present-day Christian belief. Metaphysically He is the I AM in man, the self, the directive power, raised to divine understanding and power —the I AM identity.

As the result of lack of conscious connection between the thinking faculty and the fountainhead of existence, humanity had reached a very low state. Then came Jesus of Nazareth, whose mission was to connect the thinker with the true source of thought. Thinking at random had brought man into a deplorable condition, and his salvation depended on his again joining his consciousness to the Christ. Only through that connection could he be brought back into his Edenic state—the church of God.

It is plain to any reasonable, unprejudiced mind that Jesus of Nazareth was a religious reformer with a mission from on high, that He had an insight into those things which are ever mysteries to men immersed in the sense consciousness, and that through His knowledge, and in harmony with His mission, He set into motion spiritual ideas that ever since His ministry have been operative in the world. It is evident to even a cursory reader of His life and teachings that He was the representative of a thoroughly organized plan to help men into a higher realization of God and their relation to Him.

Jesus was keenly conscious of the character of God and His own relationship to Him. He knew God as unlimited love and as ever-present, abundant life; He knew Him as wisdom and supply. He knew God as Father, who is ever ready and willing to supply every need of the human heart. He knew that as Son of God He had access to every blessing, to all the wisdom, love, and help of the Father-Mind. Jesus did not simply believe that the words He spoke were true, He knew that they were true. His words were pregnant with meaning; they were vital, living words, which carried conviction and which produced immediate results.

Jesus is the Way-Shower. He came that we might have life more abundantly; that is, He came to awaken man to the possibilities of his own nature. "As he is . . . so are we in this world (I John 4:17). He came to bear witness to Truth. He used the one true way to the realization of eternal life and the universal consciousness, therefore His influence on the race cannot be measured. It is infinite and eternal.

Jesus, crucifixion of—The Jews were under the dominion of an earth-minded priesthood. They were in a state of ignorance as regards spiritual things and did no thinking for themselves. Hence, they could not recognize or comprehend the things of which Jesus spoke to them. They were looking for a temporal king who would restore to them, by war and conquest, the earthly glory of Solomon. When Jesus tried to teach them of Spirit, of a spiritual idea, the Christ within themselves, "the hope of glory," (Col. 1:27) that would free them from every bondage of mind, body, and environment, they crucified Him.

Jesus Christ—Christ is the perfect idea of God for man. Jesus is the perfect expression of the divine idea Man. Jesus Christ is a union of the two, the idea and the expression, or in other words, He is the perfect man demonstrated.

Jesus' prayers were answered because He always dwelt in the consciousness of perfect harmony with the Father. When we ask in His name, it is with an earnest desire for that consciousness which Jesus possessed. The Christ within each of us is ever seeking perfect expression, and it should be our earnest effort to have our mind and heart clear and open channels in order that He may more perfectly work through us. When we ask in the name of Christ Jesus we ask in the consciousness that in reality we are perfect children of the Father. This harmonious relationship between God and man is attained by prayer and meditation and by constantly affirming God's presence and power. If we would have God manifest through us, we must endeavor to raise our thoughts and feelings to the standard of God.

Jew—Broadly speaking, a Hebrew. Metaphysically, a thought springing from and belonging to the praise and inner-life consciousness of the individual.

Jewess—The soul or feminine aspect of that in consciousness for which a Jew stands.

jewels—"Jewels of silver, and jewels of gold" (Exod. 12:35) represent wisdom and love in the external sense, which are to be asked for or demanded by the Children of Israel. This means that we are to affirm that all wisdom and all love, even in their most external manifestations, are spiritual. This puts Spirit in control both within and without.

John the Baptist—Represents the natural man, the physical man. His face is turned toward the light in the measure that he recognizes and pays homage to the higher self within the individual. The intellectual perception of Truth by the natural man (John the Baptist) is not the true light (the Christ) but bears witness to the light and prepares the way for its dawning in consciousness.

joy—The happiness of God expressed through His perfect idea—man. Joy and gladness are strength-giving, especially if the mind is fixed on the things of Spirit. Affirm: *"The joy of the Lord is my strength."*

Judas—Represents the ego that has possession of the sex, or life, center in the organism and is using it for its own selfish ends. Judas was a "thief." The selfish use of the life and vitality of the organism for the gratification of sense pleasure robs the higher nature, and the spiritual man is not built up. This is the betrayal of Christ.

judgment—Mental act of evaluation through comparison or contrast. Spiritual discernment; the inner voice through whose expression we come into a larger realization of ourselves.

Judgment is a faculty of the mind that can be exercised in two ways—from sense perception or spiritual understanding. If its action be based on sense perception its conclusions are fallible and often condemnatory; if based on spiritual understanding, they are safe.

judgment, day of—That period in man's development when the law of justice and righteousness begins to be felt in his consciousness, and he finds himself in the midst of experiences where he must learn the law and conform to it.

The great judgment day of Scripture indicates a time

of separation between the true and the false. There is no
warrant for the belief that God sends man to everlasting
punishment. Modern interpreters of the Bible say that the
"hell of fire" (Matt. 5:22) referred to by Jesus means
simply a time in which purification is taking place.

judgment seat—The "judgment-seat" (Rom. 14:10)
is within man. A judging, or discerning between the true
and the false, is going on daily in us as overcomers; we are
daily reaping the results of our thoughts and our deeds.

justice—When judgment is divorced from love, and
works from the head alone, there goes forth the human
cry for justice. In his mere human judgment man is hard
and heartless; he deals out punishment without consideration of motive or cause, and justice goes awry. When
justice and love meet at the heart center, there are balance,
poise, and righteousness.

There is an infinite law of justice that may be called
into activity. When we call our inner forces into action,
the universal law begins its great work in us, and all the
laws both great and small fall into line and work for us.
The true way to establish justice is by appealing directly to
the divine law.

K

karma—"The whole ethical consequence of one's acts
considered as fixing one's lot in the future existence"
(Webster). The accumulated effects of the sins of past
lives; the burden that those who believe in karma expect
to carry for ages, or until they work out of it. They are
weary treadmill travelers from birth to death, and from
death to birth. There is no such hopeless note in the teachings of Jesus. He came to bring a full consciousness of
abundant life, complete forgiveness, redemption from all
sin, and victory over death and the grave, thus delivering

man from any occasion for re-embodiment and from all bondage to karma.

"keep my word"—(John 8:51). Treasure the words of Jesus as a saving balm in time of need.

"keys of the kingdom of heaven"—(Matt. 16:19). Affirmation and denial. (see *affirmation; denial*)

king (righteous)—The executive faculty in every man whose life is guided, governed, and directed by Spirit.

"king of the Jews, this is the"—(Luke 23:38). This means that the word of the I AM goes forth as a ruling suggestion in the spiritual and intellectual. In the physical is goes forth in the individual consciousness, but the doing away with the limitations of mortal mind pulls down all walls of partition, and the whole man accepts the word of Truth.

kingdom of God—The Christ consciousness, kingdom of heaven.

kingdom of heaven—The kingdom of heaven is the realm of divine ideas, producing their expression, perfect harmony. It is within man.

kingdom within—That realm in man's consciousness where he knows and understands God.

knowing—There is in man a knowing capacity transcending intellectual knowledge. Nearly everyone has at some time touched this hidden wisdom and has been more or less astonished at its revelations. The knowing that man receives from the direct fusion of the Mind of God with his mind is real spiritual knowing.

knowledge—"Acquaintance with fact; hence, scope of information" (Webster). Intellectual knowledge is independent of feeling; it is literal knowledge without consideration of the Spirit. Man can store up a great fund of knowledge gleaned from books and teachers, but the most unlettered man who sits at the feet of his Lord in the silence comes forth radiant with the true knowledge, that of Spirit.

L

lack—"Fact or state of being deficient or wanting" (Webster). In the great Mind of Spirit there is no thought of lack. Such a thought has no rightful place in man's mind. Deny all thoughts of lack; affirm God's ever-present abundance in all your affairs.

ladder, Jacob's—Represents the step-by-step realization by means of which man assimilates the divine ideas of Truth that come to him from Jehovah.

lamb—Represents innocent, guileless forms of life on the animal plane of consciousness.

lamb, killed and eaten in the night—Represents the giving up of the animal life propensity in the mortal body. The command is that the lamb shall be without spot or blemish, and be wholly eaten after being roasted with fire. This refers to the complete transmutation and sur-render of the human life to Spirit after it has been puri-fied by the fires of regeneration.

Lamb of God—The pure life and substance of Being. By His overcoming Jesus restored to mankind the con-sciousness of this pure life and substance, which flows into man's consciousness through the spiritual body. Its nature is to vivify with perpetual life all things that it touches. Jesus is called "the Lamb of God" (John 1:29).

language—An arbitrary arrangement of sounds used to express thoughts. Thus the same thought in the minds of two men may be beyond their power to communicate to each other because they are not familiar with the intel-lect's provincial dialect. If these men were conscious of the mental plane where images are the basis of language, they would have no trouble in communicating though they were born of diverse races. The image of a horse in one mind would be seen by the other mind instantly, and communi-cation be easy. The common language of mankind is based on thought images. We shall never realize the universal language that is the dream of the philologist until we have dropped the arbitrary word plane and ascended into the realm of thought images.

laver—Basin or bowl. The laver with water therein is the word of denial ever at hand ready to cleanse every impure thought that comes into consciousness.

law—The faculty of the mind that holds every thought and act strictly to the Truth of Being, regardless of circumstances or environment. Law is a mathematical faculty. It places first things first.

Laws of mind are just as exact and undeviating as the laws of mathematics. To recognize this is the starting point in finding God.

Man does not make the law; the law is, and it was established for our benefit before the world was formed. Back of the judge is the law out of which he reads. Laws, whether natural or artificial, are but the evidence of an unseen power.

The development of man is under law. Creative mind is not only law, but is governed by the action of the law that it sets up. We have thought that man was brought forth under the fiat or edict of the great creative Mind that can make or unmake at will, or change its mind and declare a new law at any time. But a clear understanding of ourselves and of the unchangeableness of Divine Mind makes us realize that everything has its foundation in a rule of action, a law, that must be observed by both creator and created.

law, all-providing—God is the all-providing law. He is the spiritual substance out of which is made everything the race needs; the Father who supplies all His children bountifully out of His own abundance.

God is Mind; man, the offspring of God, is mind. To know the law of God, man must adjust his mind to God-Mind. The first step in applying this law is recognition of it as Truth. Unless God is known as the source of all supply, men look to the material world for support. This violates the law and breaks the connection with the one Source of all good.

law, divine—Divine law is the orderly working out of the principles of Being, or the divine ideals, into expression and manifestation throughout creation. Man, by keeping the law of right thought, works in perfect harmony with divine law, and thus paves his way into spiritual consciousness.

Divine law cannot be broken. It holds man responsible for the result of his labors. It is revealed to the mind of man through his consciously thinking on spiritual ideas.

The law that Moses laid down for the Children of Israel was one of denial and affirmation, principally denial. The law that Jesus gave was one of affirmation and love. So in taking control of the forces within, keep on the affirmative side. Let the preponderance of your thought be positive, and do not spend much time saying, *"I am not."* You may find it helpful sometimes to say, *"I am not afraid,"* but more often you should say, *"I am bold, fearless, courageous."*

law, evolutionary—Upward trend of all things; in the individual the rising of man from sense consciousness to spiritual consciousness. This law is set into action by our thinking and is continually supported by our thoughts.

law, generic—The law that operates in each group; that from which anything springs; the germ seed that brings forth after its kind.

law, mortal—The law of limitation that man has made for himself.

law, natural—The law of seed, cultivation, and harvest that natural man is subject to for the provision of his wants.

law of attraction—The law that all conditions and circumstances in affairs and body are attracted to us to accord with the thoughts we hold steadily in consciousness.

law of conservation—Building up a large reserve consciousness of substance, life, strength, and power, instead of laying up material treasures. This is done through prayer.

"Lay not up for yourselves treasures upon the earth, where moth and rust consume, and where thieves break through and steal: but lay up for yourselves treasures in heaven, where neither moth nor rust doth consume, and where thieves do not break through nor steal" (Matt. 6: 19, 20).

law of giving and receiving—The law of substance that equalizes all things. To realize and maintain divine order, substance must have both an inlet and an outlet in consciousness, and must be kept moving.

To demonstrate substance as supply, the law governing it must be recognized and kept. Those who, from pride or ignorance, do not open themselves to the inflow of substance do not demonstrate supply, and all who by selfishness refuse it an outlet, also fail. Everyone must receive freely and give as freely as he receives. Disregard of the basic principle of supply frequently hinders man's realization of the divine good. Readiness to give and readiness to receive are equally essential.

law of infinite expansion—The principle of never-ceasing growth and development toward the fulfillment of God's perfect idea that is firmly fixed in all creation.

law of justice—Many persons doubt that there is an infinite law of justice working in all things. Let them now take heart and know that this law has not worked in their affairs previously because they have not "called" it into activity at the creative center of consciousness. (see *justice*)

law of righteousness—The law of spiritual and mental growth that is raising man from sense consciousness to spiritual consciousness. The nature of the universe is purity and goodness. By abiding in the Christ consciousness, man aligns himself with this divine law. He becomes the "light of the world" (Matt. 5:14).

law of sin and death—A misnomer. Sin and death are contrary to the law of love and life. They are false beliefs endowed with power through man's erroneous thinking. This seeming law can be transcended by application of the higher and true law of immutable good. Law is Truth, and in Truth all is good. There is no Truth and no reality in sin.

law of thought purification—A rule of mind action whereby man overcomes "the world, the flesh, and the devil" by building the pure Christ consciousness.

law, transgression of—Thinking thoughts that violate the principle of harmony inherent in Being. Such transgression is followed by evil conditions. Through the strength, power, purity, and love that Jesus imparted to the race mind, we can rise superior to the penalty of transgressed law and live forever in our present body forms made glorious.

law written in our "inward parts"—A law either in or around the cells, that controls their formation and duplicates the pattern laid down ages ago in mother Eve and father Adam. "I will put my law in their inward parts, and in their heart will I write it; and I will be their God, and they shall be my people" (Jer. 31:33).

"Lazarus, come forth"—(John 11:43). This refers to the power of the Word to arouse mind energy to such an extent that the physical becomes immersed in the healing life, enabling the spiritually perfect man to come into manifestation.

leaven—The leaven is the Truth. "The kingdom of heaven is like unto leaven, which a woman took, and hid in three measures of meal, till it was all leavened" (Matt. 13:33). When a word of Truth seems to be hidden in the mind, it is not idle but is quietly spreading from point to point. This process continues until the whole consciousness is vitalized by Spirit.

"Take heed, beware of the leaven of the Pharisees and the leaven of Herod" (Mark 8:15). In this case, the leaven represents limited thoughts. When we attempt to confine the divine law to the customary avenues of expression and scoff at anything beyond, we are letting the leaven of the Pharisees work in us. When we allow the finer forces of the body to fulfill lust and appetite, we are letting the leaven of Herod work to our undoing.

"Wherefore let us keep the feast, not with old leaven, neither with the leaven of malice and wickedness, but with the unleavened bread of sincerity and truth" (I Cor. 5:8).

letting go of the old—Erasing from consciousness thoughts contrary to Truth. This is done by denial.

liberation—We are not to be liberated through suppression of sense or by violent overcoming; but through a steady, step-by-step demonstration over every error.

life—That expression of Being which manifests as animation, activity, vigor. Life and substance are ideas in Divine Mind. Life is the acting principle; substance is the thing acted upon. In the phenomenal world, life is the energy that propels all forms to action. Life is not in itself intelligent; it requires the directive power of an entity that knows where and how to apply its force in order to get the best results.

In order to give man a body having life in itself, God had to endow him with a focal life center, located in the generative organs. This center of activity in the organism is also the seat of sensation, which is the most subtle and enticing of all factors that enter into being. But these qualities (sensation and generation) are necessary to man's character, and without them he would not be the complete representative, or image and likeness, of God.

Life does not emanate from the mind; it is not a

psychic or purely mental quality, nor does it spring from the physical. Life is divine, spiritual, and its source is God, Spirit. The river of life is within man in his spiritual consciousness. He comes into consciousness of the river of life through the quickening of Spirit. He can be truly quickened with new life and vitalized in mind and body only by consciously contacting Spirit. This contact is made through prayer, meditation, and good works.

life, crown of—Living eternally in the presence of God. Its attainment depends on the understanding of the science of right thinking.

life, higher—The higher life is a higher state of mind. We know it when we realize I AM the Son of God.

lifted up in consciousness—Resurrected. One who has discovered the Truth of Being is raised, lifted up in consciousness, resurrected daily out of his old, subconscious, negative thought condition into the one positive Reality.

light—The understanding principle in mind. In divine order it always comes first into consciousness. Light is a symbol of wisdom. When Jesus said, "I am the light of the world" (John 8:12), He meant that He was the expresser of Truth in all its aspects.

light, inner—The illumination of Spirit resident in the center of every man's being.

lightning—Represents force, light, power. Jesus said, "Think not that I came to destroy the law or the prophets: I came not to destroy, but to fulfill" (Matt. 5:17); that is, He came to demonstrate that natural and spiritual law are one. He foresaw this very period when "the powers of the heavens shall be shaken" (Matt. 24:29)—that is, the mental realms were to be broken up—and He attributed this phenomenon to the coming of the Christ as "lightning."

limitation—Thoughts in consciousness that are narrow or restricted and which keep one in bondage to error. Belief in lack, illness, sin, or death are limitations in consciousness.

lion—"And one of the elders saith unto me, Weep not; behold, the Lion that is of the tribe of Judah, the Root of David, hath overcome to open the book and the seven seals thereof" (Rev. 5:5). The lion symbolizes courage, fearlessness, initiative, life. We must have the courage to enter fearlessly into the overcoming life and into the understanding of things. But courage alone will not do. We must have reverence of spiritual things—a devotional attitude—in order to receive spiritual inspiration. The phrase, "of the tribe of Judah," bespeaks this reverential nature and attitude.

lips, sinful—Lips that utter faultfinding words, condemnatory words. The law is, "The lips of the wise shall preserve them" (Prov. 14:3).

logic—(derived from the word *Logos*, which see). A rational relation or connection between idea and expression. Logic in its strictest sense is the only accurate method of arriving at Truth. Any system of philosophy or religious doctrine that does not admit of the rules of perfect logic in reaching its conclusion from a stated premise, must be outside the pale of pure reason and in the realm of man-made dogma. *Logic* and *Logos* are almost synonymous terms, and the highest scriptural authority tells us that all things were made by the Word. Hence, the word of reason or the reasonable word is the very foundation of the universe. Therefore, to know accurately about the reality of things we must disregard all appearances as indicated by the five senses, and go into pure reason—the Spirit from which was created everything that has permanent existence.

Logos—The Word of God; the divine archetype idea that contains all ideas: the Christ, the Son of God, spiritual man in manifestation. Divine Mind in action. This supreme idea is the creative power, the Christ consciousness formulated by universal Principle.

Logos, law of the—The law of divine creation produces the order and harmony of perfect thought. Law puts first things first. It is a rule of action.

An understanding of the Logos reveals to us the law under which all things are brought forth, the law of mind action. Divine Mind creates by thought, through ideas.

Lord—The activity of the spiritual I AM as the ruling consciousness. The Lord God of the Scriptures is Christ, the Spiritual Man; our divine consciousness; the creative power within us.

Lord, absence from—A state in which both mind and body are functioning in carnality.

Lord is One, the—Oneness of thought and purpose in the individual, as well as the one Presence and one Power—the omnipotent good, which man must know and consider in his contact with the world without. The principle of oneness controls life.

Lord, wrath of the—(see *wrath of God*)

Lord's Prayer—A series of ideas illustrative of man's relationship to his Creator.

Lord's Supper—(Matt. 26:26-30). Metaphysically, God's covenant with mankind, through His perfect idea, Christ Jesus. This compact was completed through Jesus' breaking the bread and blessing the cup. The bread symbolizes spiritual substance, or the body. The wine symbolizes the blood of Jesus, or spiritual life.

We eat the body of Jesus by affirming the one spiritual substance to be the substance of our body and we drink His blood by affirming and realizing our oneness with the one divine, omnipresent life of Spirit.

love—The pure essence of Being that binds together the whole human family. Of all the attributes of God, love is undoubtedly the most beautiful. In Divine Mind, love is the power that joins and binds in divine harmony the universe and everything in it; the great harmonizing principle known to man.

Divine love is impersonal; it loves for the sake of loving. It is not concerned with what or who it loves, nor with a return of love. Like the sun, its joy is in the shining forth of its nature. "Love suffereth long, *and* is kind; love envieth not; love vaunteth not itself, is not puffed up" (I Cor. 13:4).

Love is an inner quality that sees good everywhere and in everybody. It insists that all is good, and by refusing to see anything but good it causes that quality finally to appear uppermost in itself, and in all things.

Love is the great harmonizer and healer. Whoever calls on God as Holy Spirit for healing is calling on divine love. Divine love will bring your own to you, adjust all misunderstandings, and make your life and affairs healthy, happy, harmonious, and free, "Love therefore is the fulfilment of the law" (Rom. 13:10).

luck—All things come about through law. Men sometimes blindly keep the law or part of it for a time, and it works for them. Not understanding the cause that produced their success, they call it "luck" and build up a belief in "chance."

lust of the flesh—Sense consciousness, which causes man to be tempted. So long as he is ruled by the serpent of sense, man is not fulfilling divine law. The activity of the cleansing, refining process of Spirit is hindered in man when he lets lustful desire enter the love consciousness.

M

magnify the Lord—The mind possesses magnifying power, which it exercises habitually, either consciously or unconsciously. This power makes the mind the fertile side of man's nature, out of which spring "the issues of life." We magnify the Lord by anticipation, by expecting, by declaring that only the good is true, by steadfastly declaring that every blessing is ours now.

malefactors, crucified with Jesus—Represent duality—belief in good and evil, past and future—comprising all the thought consciousness of opposites that has been built up since man began to eat, or enter into the conscious knowledge of "good and evil" (Gen. 2:17).

mammon—Treasure; wealth; the material or worldly thought and belief regarding riches, possessions, and wealth, compared with the true inner riches of the mind, which are the understanding and the realization of the spiritual substance, life, and intelligence that lie back of every outer manifestation.

man—An idea in Divine Mind; the epitome of being. The apex of God's creation, created in His image and likeness.

Man appears unlike God because he, through disobedience, fell into sin. Through accepting race thoughts, man has adopted wrong ideas about himself and his relation to his Source. He has believed that he is unlike God and separate from Him, and these concepts have, by the law of thought, become manifest.

Ideal man is the perfect man, the Christ, the offspring of Divine Mind. Manifest man should be as perfect as the ideal, and he will be when the individual identifies himself with the Christ. When he is identified with anything less than perfection he manifests some degree of imperfection.

Man makes his world through the activity of ideas in his consciousness—ideas of wisdom, power, intelligence. The real man is the embodiment of God, and all the God-substance and the power to make it active is inherent within him.

When we are quickened to spiritual understanding and fully realize the true character of God and our own nature as the image, or idea, of God we will begin to live as Jesus lived in order that we may bring forth the likeness. To perceive the true character of God and His attributes and then to grasp our relationship to Him is to realize that His attributes are our attributes, His power is our power; His character is our character.

man, age of—Man is not limited in life. He has existed with the Father always. At the very beginning of creation he was born into being through the Son, the Christ, the perfect, ideal man whom God made in His image and likeness.

"Jesus said . . . Before Abraham was born, I am" (John 8:58).

man, duality of—Man is a duality in seeming only. He is a unit when he knows himself. His ignorance of himself and his relation to God is the cause of the seeming duality. When wisdom comes to him and he makes wisdom his own, there is no longer war between the ideal man in God and the becoming man in the Lord God.

man, fall of—The result that follows man's failure to recognize his divinity. By his error he falls into a state of consciousness where he is bound in limitation and error. He falls short of his divine possibilities.

man idea—Before there could be a man there must have been an idea of man. God, the Father, Divine Mind, had an idea of man, and this idea is his Son, the perfect man idea, the offspring of God-Mind. This Son is the Christ, the only begotten of the Father. The Son, being the express image and likeness of the Father, is perfect, even as the Father which is in heaven is perfect. All that we find in Divine Mind we find in its offspring, "who is the image of the invisible God, the firstborn of all creation" (Col. 1:15). "In him dwelleth all the fulness of the Godhead bodily" (Col. 2:9).

man, illumined intellectual—John the Baptist represents the illumined intellectual man who perceives with spiritual vision the unfoldment of this natural, intellectual man into the Christ man.

man, mortal—An error concept or expression of man, a misunderstanding of his true nature that results in an untrue expression of God-given powers and ends in death.

man, new—(Eph. 4:24; Col. 3:10). The "new man" is born of a divine idea through the overshadowing of the Holy Spirit. This idea is that man is a spiritual being; he is a "holy thing."

man of sin—The "man of sin" is the carnal mind in each individual, and it always opposes and misrepresents the Truth; sometimes it poses as an angel of light and Truth. Everyone who overcomes this inner adversary will be saved from all deception that may be practiced by anybody or anything that claims the place of the Lord Jesus Christ.

man, sense—The earth man, who lives through his senses. He gathers his information and makes his judgments from evidence gathered by the senses. He seeks his pleasure through the satisfaction of his sense appetites. He is the false man, the antichrist man.

man, Son of—Unregenerate man; personality, the name of the personal consciousness. The spiritual man is God's Son; the personal man is man's son.

man, spiritual—The sum total of the attributes or perfect idea of Being, identified and individualized. This man is the "only begotten Son" (John 3:16) of God.

Jehovah, or "I AM THAT I AM" (Exod. 3:14), is the name of this divine man. He was manifested as the higher self of Jesus. In the New Testament He is called the Christ. Jesus named Him the "Father in me" (John 14:10). He called Him Father more than forty times.

man, ungodly—The ungodly man is unlike God; he seeks to accumulate material riches, to gain worldly knowledge or fame. He does not know God as the prosperity of himself and all others. "But the way of the wicked [ungodly] shall perish" (Psalms 1:6).

manna—The bread of life; the Word of God. Represents the realization that the divine substance is everywhere present, in every part of the consciousness.

manger—Represents the animal life of the body in which the new life is first manifested.

manifestation—The materialization of a Truth idea; the coming forth into visibility of that which has been affirmed; the appearance of an idea.

mansions, many—(John 14:2). Degrees of realization of the Truth of Being. The "place" that Jesus prepared is a definite state of realization of Truth into which may come all who take up the same denials and affirmations that He took up.

mantle of Elijah—Represents the reflected power that falls on us and becomes the abiding part of our consciousness, after we have declared the Truth in the highest until it makes visible the mental currents ("chariots") and vital powers ("horsemen") of Being (II Kings 2:12).

mark on Cain—The mark set on Cain to keep him from being slain was the consciousness of his divine origin. No matter how deep in transgressions the body may be, it still bears the stamp of God.

marriage, spiritual—Spiritually, marriage represents the union of two dominant states of consciousness. When we open the door of the mind by consciously affirming the presence and power of the divine I AM in our midst, there is a marriage or union of the higher forces in being with the lower and we find that we are quickened in every part; the life of the I AM has been poured out for us.

masters—Certain persons who call themselves "masters" claim that they have forged ahead of the race in their understanding and use of some of the powers of mind and have in personal egotism set up kingdoms and put themselves on thrones. These so-called "masters" and members of occult brotherhoods are attracting susceptible minds away from the straight and narrow path and leading them to believe that there is a short cut into the kingdom. Jesus described the situation forcibly and clearly in Matthew 24:24: "For there shall arise false Christs, and false prophets, and shall show great signs and wonders; so as to lead astray, if possible, even the elect."

mastery and dominion—We demonstrate mastery and dominion by persistently thinking thoughts of power and strength in the absolute principle of Truth, and through the I AM establishing them in our own consciousness.

materiality—The concept that the material universe is real, that the three-dimension world really exists. The truth is that the material world is a limitation of the four-dimension world; it has no permanent existence and will come to an end. This is attested to by both religion and science.

matter—Man's limited concept of divine substance that he has "formed" in consciousness; a thought of substance as dense, solid, weighty, and separate from the spiritual life that underlies it. When man is quickened of the Spirit he knows Spirit to be all, in all, and he gives all thought to this reality.

matter, rule of—That state of man where material ideas and standards are the established rule of his life and actions.

meat eating—Meat eating stimulates the sense man and interferes with the development of spiritual power. For many reasons it is better to abstain from a meat diet.

First, because of the command, "Thou shalt not kill" (Exod. 20:13). Injustice and cruelty react on the one who practices them, whether he himself kills or partakes of that which has been killed for him by others. Meat eating requires the spilling of blood, which destroys Truth in consciousness. Destructive ideas are introduced into the stomach, producing doubts and fears and physical inharmonies. The love of God should be expressed toward all animals.

meditation—Continuous and contemplative thought; to dwell mentally on anything; realizing the reality of the Absolute; a steady effort of the mind to know God; man's spiritual approach to God.

The purpose of meditation is to expand the consciousness Christward; to bring into realization divine Truth; to be transformed in spirit, soul, and body by the renewing of the mind.

meek, the—Anyone highly trained to react to all negative stimuli with love instead of with "an eye for an eye." "Blessed are the meek: for they shall inherit the earth" (Matt. 5:5).

men of Israel—The religious thoughts and aspirations of man, which give him access to resurrection life through faith in the Christ.

men of valor, mighty—Strong, courageous, conquering thoughts expressed by man, inspired by the establishment of praise (Judah) and faith (Benjamin) in consciousness.

mental assimilation—The mind assimilates what it affirms.

mental atmosphere—Surrounding or prevailing mental influence. Your mental attitude, thoughts, and words are creative or destructive influences in your world.

mental discipline—The practice of the daily training of the mind through denials of error and affirmations of Truth.

mental premise—A basic mental premise is an original

proposition of Truth that serves as the ground for affirmation, such as, *"All is good."*

mentality, adverse—The mortal mind with its beliefs and thoughts opposed to the perfect Mind of Christ is the adverse mentality. All sin, suffering, disease, and death are the work of the adverse mentality.

merchant—One who is seeking the "jewel" of spiritual good, through exchange of thought, discussion, and argument. In order to attain the inner pearl, the unadulterated Truth, man must give up the so-called values and realize his oneness with the Christ within.

mercy—Christlike treatment toward the suffering. The important point in desiring to be merciful is righteous adjustment, as this results in true overcoming.

messenger—An intellectual perception of Truth that cleanses the mind and heart and leads to the coming or conscious presence of the indwelling Spirit of truth, the Christ.

messengers of God—Spiritual thoughts that always bring messages of light and point the way to a harmonious co-operation between the indwelling love of the heart and the understanding of the head.

Messiah—The promise of the visible manifestation of the Christ. Christ is the fulfillment in man of this promise.

metaphysician—One skilled in the science of Being; a student and teacher of the laws of Spirit.

metaphysics—The systematic study of the science of Being; that which transcends the physical. By pure metaphysics is meant a clear understanding of the realm of ideas and their legitimate expression.

microbes, how formed—Microbes or germs are formed by the power of thought. Thoughts become entities and have identity according to the character of the thought in the mind of the thinker. Error thoughts make disease microbes. Positive thoughts form intelligent body-builders.

middle wall of partition—The division between the

conscious mind and the subconscious mind, caused by man's lack of understanding of his true I AM nature. This partition is broken down by the realization and manifestation of the one Divine Mind.

midnight—The darkened negative state of consciousness.

millennium—Man has for untold ages looked forward to a millennium day. That day will always be in the future until we let go of our thought of a future. The millennium day is now. It is established today—this very hour.

millstone—A seeming hindrance of an earthly nature; a heavy burden.

Mind—By the term *Mind,* we mean God—the universal Principle, which includes all principles.

As an aid in understanding how the universal Mind creates, we can observe the action of our own mind because we are the offspring of the one Mind and we bring forth in like manner. "The Son can do nothing of himself, but what he seeth the Father doing: for what things soever he doeth, these the Son also doeth in like manner" (John 5:19).

Man in the consciousness of the one Mind has no sense of apartness. Through affirmation he can attune himself to Being, transmute his thoughts into ideas, and accomplish the seemingly impossible.

mind—The starting point of every act and thought and feeling; the common meeting ground of God and man. God is mind, and we cannot describe God with human language, so we cannot describe mind. We can only say: I am mind; I know. God is mind; He knows.

The mind is the seat of perception of the things we see, hear, and feel. It is through the mind that we see the beauties of the earth and sky, of music, of art, in fact, of everything. That silent shuttle of thought working in and out through cell and nerve weaves into one harmonious whole the myriad moods of mind, and we call it life.

mind, affirmative state of—A binding, holding process. If man affirms his unity with the life, substance, and intelligence of God, he lays hold of these spiritual qualities.

mind, carnal—Misuse of mind powers, arising from ignorance of the relationship between God and man. A state of consciousness formed about a false ego or false concept of man. All the "works of the flesh" (Gal. 5:19) are the product of carnal mind.

mind, change of—A change of mind is the very first requisite of the new life in Christ. We go into this new and higher state of consciousness as we would go into another country. The kingdom of heaven is right here in our midst and will become tangible reality to us when we have developed the faculties necessary to comprehend it.

mind, fixed state of—A combination of thoughts in consciousness that is hard to change; ideas that have crystallized.

mind, mortal—Error consciousness in unregenerate man, or man composed of ungodlike thoughts. It is the opposite of the Christ Mind, which is the perfect Mind of God in man. Mortal mind gathers its information through the senses. It judges by appearances, which are often false judgments. Man must renounce this false state of mind if he is to be one with God. Mortal mind breeds sin, poverty, sickness, and death.

mind of the flesh—(Rom. 8:7) Mixed thoughts, selfishness, fear, and the like. These thoughts are what we find in persons of Gentile consciousness, and in the regeneration they must be eliminated.

mind, subconscious—The sum of all man's past thinking; also his memory. The subconscious mind sometimes acts as though separate from the conscious mind: for instance, in dreams. The subconscious mind has no power to do original thinking. It can act only upon what is given to it through the conscious or the superconscious mind.

mind, three phases of—Conscious mind, subconscious mind, and superconscious mind, called the Lord. The superconscious mind transcends both the conscious and subconscious phases of mind. The harmonious working together of these three seemingly separate minds is necessary to the bringing forth of the latent possibilities of man.

miracle—"An event or effect in the physical world beyond or out of the ordinary course of things, deviating from the known laws of nature, or transcending our knowledge of these laws" (Webster). In reality miracles are events that take place as a result of the operation of a higher, unknown law. All true action is governed by law. Nothing just happens. All happenings are the result of cause and can be explained under the law of cause and effect.

Mighty things have been wrought in the past by those who had mere blind faith to guide them. To faith we now add understanding of the law, and our achievements will be a fulfillment of the promise of Jesus, "He that believeth on me, the works that I do shall he do also; and greater *works* than these shall he do" (John 14:12).

mist—Lack of clear understanding between the earth consciousness and the spiritual Mind.

money—A medium of exchange and a measurement of value. The materialization of spiritual substance. The symbol of the idea of prosperity.

Money is a symbol that represents values in goods, land, or service. Substance in the form of money is given to us for constructive uses. The money idea is good and draws to us good when we are functioning in divine order.

Love of money is the root of much evil. Man should love the source of all money, God.

money changers—Dishonest thoughts of materialism and greed. The consciousness must be cleansed of these if the body temple is to be kept pure and holy.

moon—Represents personal intelligence; the intellect. Its light is supplied by the sun, symbol of spiritual light.

mortal beliefs—Beliefs in sickness, sin, poverty, trouble, accident, and death, which are prevalent in the race mind.

mortal consciousness—Consciousness of self as separate from God. This is a false consciousness. Consciousness must harmonize with God-Mind to be free from thoughts of poverty, sin, sickness, and death.

mortal ego—Identification of the I AM with the whole array of false race and individual mental patterns.

mortal plane—That realm of ideas conceived in mortal, or material consciousness.

mortal words—Words spoken by the intellectual man. They are empty because they lack the life and substance necessary to impart spiritual life and nourishment to the mind.

motherhood, divine—The brooding, nourishing element of Divine Mind, or God, in which spiritual ideals are brought to fruition.

mountain—A mountain represents an exalted state of mind where the divine plan may be perceived and unfolded; a state of spiritual realization.

The "high mountain" to which personality carries us in our spiritual uplift is the consciousness of power over mortal thought in all its earthly avenues of expression. Going up into the mountain to pray means elevating our thoughts and our aspirations to the spiritual viewpoint.

mule—Represents human will. When it is ridden and is obedient, it infers subjection of that faculty to the established order.

multitude—The "great multitude" of John 6:5 is composed of our own hungry thoughts. They want an influx of the Truth of Spirit into consciousness. "Man doth not live by bread only, but by everything that proceedeth out of the mouth of Jehovah doth man live" (Deut. 8:3).

mustard seed—The mustard seed comparison shows the capacity of the apparently small thought of Truth to develop in consciousness until it becomes the abiding place of a higher range of thoughts (birds of the air).

myrrh—An aromatic gum resin; a slightly pungent perfume, used for incense. Metaphysically myrrh represents the eternity of Spirit, an emblem of the Resurrection, an ointment of love.

mystic—One who has intimate, firsthand acquaintance with God; a man of prayer. Jesus was the greatest mystic of all ages.

mysticism—The practice of the presence of God; the life of prayer that results in intuitive knowledge and experience of God.

The Bible contains more high mysticism than all other books. Spiritual things are spiritually discerned. It is necessary to call on one's own spiritual light to enter into the deep mysticism of the Bible.

N

name—An arbitrary appellation received in the language of the intellect describing a mental image or thought picture.

In the English language we have a very careless way of expressing the recondite meaning of words, but in the Hebrew the name of every person or thing represents its character. Every name in the Scriptures has an inner meaning. For instance, *Bethlehem* means "house of bread," and indicates the nerve center at the pit of the stomach through which the universal substance joins with the refined or spiritualized chemical products of the body substance.

The Scriptures give much importance to the naming and numbering of the prophets and peoples. The Lord always gave the wise men and leaders new names when they achieved some signal victory. The record abounds with such examples. When the great Jehovah sent Moses to bring the Children of Israel out of Egypt He gave the name by which He was to be known: "I AM THAT I AM."

name, God's—To describe God is to give Him limitation, hence He could not be given a fairer designation than "I AM THAT I AM." This is without confines or bounds and it allows unlimited expansion in every direction.

Metaphysicians have found that this name held in mind persistently gives the mind freedom from narrow beliefs. It lets the imagination soar away from its dimensional concepts of God, and there flows into the mind in consequence a whole flood of expanded ideas.

name of Jesus—Spiritual understanding proves that the name of a great character carries his name potency and that wherever his name is repeated silently or audibly his attributes become manifest. Jesus knew this, and He commanded His disciples to go forth in His name. The marvelous healing works that they did in His name prove the great spiritual power resident in His name.

napkin—Represents that in which something is hid. Too often we keep concealed a bit of Truth or a talent that should be taken out and put to some good use. (see Luke 19:20)

narrow door—The open mind that measures all things by the gauge of Truth. This way is "straitened" because it requires that only Truth be recognized, and it rules out untruth or evil.

nations—Aggregations of thoughts in the mind that are to be instructed through the faculties.

nature—The intellect's name for God. Men fall short when they seek to find God by studying nature. Instead of molding and animating the cells of their bodies, they project thought outward in speculating about the universe and its law.

Nature is the servant of mind, and when lawful thoughts are enthroned in consciousness nature restores the natural harmony existing between Spirit, soul, and body. When man asserts his divine supremacy he dominates nature.

nature, animal—The undisciplined nature in man or that phase of his being which has been allowed to express according to the desires of sense.

nature, restorative power of—This is the name given by doctors to the Spirit of health, which is always right at hand awaiting an opportunity to enter in to make whole and to harmonize all discords in the body.

neck—The seat of the power faculty in man.

necromancy—An activity of man's mind used adversely in which he is in league with hidden forces such as mesmerism and black magic and uses them in selfish ways.

negation—The unreal; that which has no basis in reality.

negative—The state of consciousness that repels good and attracts its own likeness, lack. Poverty is the negative side of plenty; sickness is the negative side of health; death is the negative side of life. These states result from the mind's being allowed to image anything contrary or adverse to the one almighty resource, God.

negative, dealing with—Denial of error thoughts and beliefs.

nerve fluid—A spiritual fluid that God is propelling throughout man's whole being continually, as the electromagnetic center of every physically expressed atom. This wonderful stream of nerve fluid finds its way over all the nerves in man's body temple, giving him the invigorating, steadying power of the Holy Spirit.

nerves—"Cordlike or filamentous bands of nervous tissue that connect parts of the nervous system with the other organs of the body, and conduct nervous impulses to or away from these organs" (Webster). The nerves have been described as wires over which messages are sent to and from the brain. Every emotion and every feeling that is transmitted over the nerves to the brain is registered and translated into thought, which may be expressed through the spoken word.

net—Man's mind is the net that catches thoughts, which are the basis of external conditions. This net works hard and long in the darkness of human understanding and gains but little, but once the Christ Mind is perceived and obeyed the net is cast on "the right side," and success follows.

new birth—The realization by man of his spiritual identity, with the fullness of power and glory that follows.

A birth is a coming into a state of being. Man first is born, or comes into a state of physical being; he thinks of himself as flesh, material. The "new birth" is the coming into a higher state of being that is alive to the fact that man is like God, one with God.

newness of life—Understanding of the spiritual facts of being.

new race—The race of men expressing the perfection of God as typified in Jesus. All men are potential members of this new race; they can become a part of it by following and demonstrating the Christ principle.

New Thought—A mental system that holds man as being one with God (good) through the power of constructive thinking.

night—Represents human understanding in which man's thought net works long and hard with little gain.

nonresistance—A passive state of mind. The law of nonresistance as taught by Jesus is demonstrated only by erasing from the individual consciousness every thought of personal rights.

nostrils—Represent openness to the inspirations of Divine Mind.

numbered—To be numbered is to be especially designated as having place, relation, importance, and necessity.
If you are numbered you are one of the factors that enter
into the great problem of life. To number and to name
mean one and the same thing. If you are numbered you
are therefore recorded in the annals of heaven and the
omnipresent Father knows you by a name peculiar to Spirit.

O

obedience, spiritual—Obedience comes through understanding man's relation to God. When we show forth wisdom and purity and the perfect Principle that is God, we
are obedient to Him.

object of man's existence—The mortal concept of the
object of man's existence is personal pleasure and profit.
The spiritual concept is to express God.

obsession—All conscious thought may become subconscious. An error may be held in mind until it is firmly
fixed or crystallized and so strong that it takes control of
a man. Such controlling mental states are false states of
consciousness. Anger, jealousy, greed, appetite, passion are
traits that, when allowed to become dominant, are obses-
sions, and are the "demons" that are to be cast out.

occultism—The belief that secret and mysterious powers can control the visible world. This procedure is not
the way of the Christ Mind. "For there is nothing hid,
save that it should be manifested; neither was *anything*
made secret, but that it should come to light" (Mark
4:22).

offerings, freewill—"Freely ye received, freely give"
(Matt. 10:8) is a law of life, and all must conform to it
in order to realize their highest good and to receive abundantly. Giving measures the receiving.

oil, anointing—The thought of love, which is poured

over anything, making it holy or a perfect whole. "Love . . . is the fulfillment of the law" (Rom. 13:10).

ointment—Symbolizes affirmation of peace, poise, and gladness.

ointment in alabaster cruse—The conserved nerve fluid that is stored up in the secret recesses of the body.

ointment, precious—Fragrance of love with which understanding (feet) is often bathed.

old age—A false belief deeply imbedded in the race mind. It accepts biological law as the ultimate for man instead of the law of God—which is eternal life in the body.

Omega—(see *Alpha and Omega*)

omnipotence—Infinite power. God is infinite power. All the power there is. All-powerful.

omnipresence—God is Mind. The one Mind contains all, and all ideas exist in the one Mind. God is everywhere present. There is no place where God is not. He is in all, through all, and around all. Omnipresence is a spiritual realm that can be penetrated only through the most highly accelerated mind action, as in prayer.

omniscience—God as omniscience is all-knowing, all-knowledge.

omniscient—All-knowing; infinite knowledge and wisdom. Divine Mind is omniscient. It knows all.

one life and one intelligence—There is one Spirit; one principle of life, love, intelligence, and goodness in, through, and over all, even God, the good omnipotent.

one Mind—There is but one Mind. Every individual and the various phases of character that make that individual are but states of consciousness in the one Mind.

one presence and one power—God, Spirit, is the only presence in the universe, and is the only power. He is in, through, and around all creation as its life and sustaining power.

one Spirit-Mind—God is the one Spirit-Mind in which

all ideas of life, love, substance, intelligence, and power originate.

opposition in consciousness—The effort of old states of mind to continue exercising dominion in the face of new ideas becoming active in mind.

optimism—The inclination to expect good; the practice of seeing God (All-Good) everywhere. A sturdy belief in the goodness of reality.

order—The divine idea of order is the idea of adjustment, and as this is established in man's thought, his mind and affairs will be at one with the universal harmony.

ordinances of Jehovah—"The ordinances of Jehovah are true, *and* righteous altogether" (Psalms 19:9). Ordinances are established rules, and here we have the divine law under a slightly different aspect. When a man keeps the law of his being, he is guided into greater sureness and definiteness of understanding.

organic regeneration—To become conscious of divine substance, affirm your unity with it until you feel it as an exquisite vibration in every part of your body. This is the baptism of the Holy Spirit so often referred to by the apostles, and when you feel it you may know that you are tasting the "hidden manna" (Rev. 2:17), that you have begun organic regeneration that will be completed in immortality in the body, "the body of Christ" (I Cor. 12:27).

organs of the body—All outward conditions are the result of ideas that have first appeared in mind. The organs of the body are bundles of ideas that have organized themselves about a working center. They have their positive pole in mind, and it is there that we should look for the means to regulate them.

"our daily bread"—(Matt. 6:11). Our daily bread is the sustenance for spirit, soul, and body. Some of this "daily bread" is appropriated in the form of food. But man does "not live by bread alone, but by every word that proceedeth out of the mouth of God" (Matt. 4:4). There is substance in words of Truth, and this substance is appropriated by prayer and meditation on Truth.

outer understanding—Man's intellectual consciousness that gathers knowledge and substance for personal advancement and gain. This is not true spiritual understanding, but is a hireling, a stranger, so far as concerns the getting of good by waiting on the inner teacher, the Spirit of truth.

overcome the world—To correct thoughts that fall short of the divine ideal.

overcomer—One who recognizes the Truth of his being and is renewing his mind and body and affairs by changing his thoughts from the old mortal beliefs to the new as he sees them in Divine Mind. He demonstrates the divine law, not only in surface life but in innermost consciousness. Spiritual power, mastery, and dominion are attained by the overcomer. "He that overcometh, I will give to him to sit down with me in my throne" (Rev. 3:21).

overcoming—"Gaining superiority; winning" (Webster). Through thought mastery, sense man is overcome. The victorious thought of love defeats the thoughts of hate and fear. "Be of good cheer; I have overcome the world" (John 16:33).

overcoming, spiritual—Dealing with the problems of life in spiritual understanding and demonstrating over error through the keeping of spiritual laws.

oversoul—The universal Principle, the absolute One, God, Being. The absolute reality. The oversoul is the divine thought man. Jesus is the expressed oversoul of this planet.

P

pagan—One in any age who believes in the power of material things.

paganism—The religion of pagans, pertaining to idolatrous worship. The worship of money as God is a form of paganism.

pain—An indication that the vital forces of the body are at work to bring about health.

palm trees—Metaphysically, realizations in the physical of unlimited resource of strength.

pantheism—"The doctrine that the universe, taken or conceived of as a whole, is God; the doctrine that there is no God but the combined forces and laws which are manifested in the existing universe" (Webster).

In its last analysis what we call nature, pantheists would name God. Metaphysically, pantheism refers to God as omnipresence, the one living, all-powerful, intelligent Mind, pervading and sustaining all things and directing them in love, wisdom, and order.

Pantheism and the teachings of Unity differ widely: pantheism diminishes the importance of the individual, while Unity teaches that man always retains his individual identity in God-Mind.

parable—A brief symbolical story told to illustrate Truth. "He taught them many things in parables" (Mark 4:2).

paradise—A state of high spiritual consciousness.

parsimony—In mortal consciousness, the idea of closeness in expenditures; undue thrift. Indicates lack of understanding of accessibility of supply through omnipresent substance.

Passover—Outwardly a Jewish feast; symbolically, a mental attitude in which we are bridging over from an old state of consciousness and entering a new. In taking on the Christ consciousness men pass over from the mortal to the spiritual consciousness.

pasture—Metaphysically, a pasture represents substance in a form in which it can be utilized by the individual. "He maketh me to lie down in green pastures" (Psalms 23).

patience—An attitude of mind characterized by poise, inner calmness, and quiet endurance, especially in the face of trying conditions. Patience has its foundation in faith, and it is perfected only in those who have unwavering faith in God. "The proving of your faith worketh patience" (James 1:3).

pattern—The divine incarnation of Jesus is the divine pattern for all men who are seeking the Christ way of life.

peace—Harmony and tranquillity derived from awareness of the Christ consciousness. "Peace I leave with you; my peace I give unto you" (John 14:27). Steadfast affirmations of peace will harmonize the whole body structure and open the way to attainment of health conditions in mind and body.

Until world peace is based on the divine law of love and this law incorporated into the pact of peace as well as into the minds of those who sign the pact, there will be no permanent peace.

peacemaker—One who has the ability to say "peace" to the turbulent waves of thought and have them obey. A peacemaker is one who reduces to peace and harmony all the thoughts of strife, anger, and retaliation in his own mind. The ability to say "peace" to thoughts, and have them obey, entitles man to sonship of the Most High. "Blessed are the peacemakers: for they shall be called sons of God" (Matt. 5:9).

pearl of great price—The Truth that no man can afford to barter away, although all the kingdoms of the earth and the glory of them be weighed in the balance against this one treasure.

Pentateuch—The first five books of the Bible, called the books of law, or the books of Moses.

Pentecost—The "day of Pentecost" was with the Israelites the great "feast of harvest," or "day of the first-fruits" (Exod. 23:16; Num. 28:26).

"That day of Pentecost" signifies a gathering of spiritual powers for the purpose of harvesting the first fruits of Spirit; otherwise, a dedicating of these new forces of Spirit to unselfish service in the vineyard of the Lord.

The first Pentecost after Jesus' ascension was the time of the first recorded coming of the Holy Spirit baptism upon His apostles and immediate followers. The descent into consciousness of the Jesus Christ life may have taken place on the day of Pentecost in the company of the apostles as described. They were in the upper room of the mind, which is a spiritual state of mind, and had been praying for ten days with one accord for the fulfillment of the promise of the Holy Spirit as given by Jesus. This attitude of many minds forms a mental magnet and brings about results in flashes of light and spiritual illumination. Religious revivals have demonstrated this to greater or lesser degree.

people, holy—The members of the body of Christ are called a holy people because they are different from the world about them in that they refer all things to the indwelling Presence. In their method of praying and of attaining health and plenty, in their manner of conversation, and in all vital points their lives are set to a higher standard than that of the people of the world.

perception, spiritual—Apprehension of Truth through intuition; the ability to perceive spiritually; the faculty of seeing spiritual reality in spite of appearances that may suggest the contrary.

perfection—A state of consciousness completely free from any shadow of negation.

perfection, attainment of—Jesus said, "Ye therefore shall be perfect, as your heavenly Father is perfect" (Matt. 5:48). We attain divine perfection through spiritual aspiration, by never ceasing to erase false thoughts and by affirming Truth as the law of our being.

perseverance—Metaphysically, to persist in pursuit of Truth. Through perseverance we make connection with the higher realms of consciousness.

persistency—The inner spiritual quality of an abiding conviction that urges one on to accomplishment. Persistency in prayer awakens the spiritual consciousness. When this awakening has been accomplished, one is in a constant state of thanksgiving and praising, and the joy of a conscious union with creative Mind is realized.

personal aims—Personal aims are concerned exclusively with one's own welfare. They are always narrow and selfish. So long as these exist and take the place of the rightful one, there is no room for the higher self, the Christ of God. "Let him deny himself . . . and follow me" (Matt. 16:24).

personal man—Adam.

personality—The sum total of characteristics that man has personalized as distinct of himself, independent of others or of divine principle. The word *personality* as used by metaphysicians is contrasted with the word *individuality*. Individuality is the real; personality is the unreal, the mortal, the part of us that is governed by the selfish motives of the natural man. (see *individuality*)

Personality is a veil or mask worn by man that conceals the real, the spiritual I AM. Jesus shattered this mask and revealed Christ, the true man of God.

Individuality is Jehovah, ideal man; image and likeness of Elohim, universal creative Mind.

Personality is Adam, man formed by Jehovah and commanded to develop his individuality in Eden, an environment of all potential possibilities.

Personality is what man seems to be when he thinks in his three-dimensional consciousness; individuality is what he really is when he thinks in his unlimited spiritual consciousness.

As the true Christ self emerges, personality decreases. The real self, the individuality, begins to express. "He must increase, but I must decrease" (John 3:30).

pessimism—An unhappy mental state resulting from beholding the shadow of reality, termed evil.

pests—All vermin and pests of every kind come from wrong thoughts and expressions of life in man and by man. God is life, and all life springs from the one perfect life-idea. Man brings the life of God into manifestation through his thoughts, words, and acts. Through ignorance and wrong thinking man has worked out of divine order with the great principle of life and has brought about the different manifestations of life that prey on and torment him today.

Pharisee—One who observes the letter of the religious law but not its spirit; lacking in understanding of the Truth.

The Pharisees were hypocrites. Jesus denounced them with greater severity than any other class of sinners. They pretended to practice the divine law, but failed to do so. They represent the son who said, "I *go,* sir; and went not" (Matt. 21:30).

Physician, the Great—The omnipresent, healing, indwelling Spirit of Jesus Christ.

pillar of cloud—Light of spiritual understanding to guide us.

pillar of fire—Witness of the Spirit on the altar of love as a glow of light that opens the understanding.

"place" that Jesus prepared—(John 14:2) Jesus said He had prepared a "place" for us. This "place" is a spiritual current in the cosmic ether in which we live, and we can feel it when we direct our attention to Jesus Christ in prayer and meditation. "The kingdom of God is nigh" (Luke 21:31).

planes—The different realms of ideas in which men function. There are many planes of life, one above or below another, yet not conflicting. All creation is based on life activity, or as it is called in physical science, rates of vibration. A certain activity in the life current forms worlds on a plane, which we may call the physical; a little increase in the vibratory rate makes another system, which we may designate as the psychical; a still higher rate makes a universe where spiritual ideas prevail.

These are all interlaced and interblended in the presence around and within us, hence the "kingdom of God is within you" (Luke 17:21), or "among you," as one translator gives it.

plumb line—The divine law that measures uprighteousness or integrity.

poise—A state of consciousness that beholds the world from the harmony of the Christ Mind; a freedom from personal thinking.

pool—Metaphysically, the realization in consciousness that our life is being constantly purified, healed, and made new by the activity of mind.

poor in spirit—Those who have denied personal consciousness. They are poor in the spirit of selfishness, but rich in the Spirit of Christ. "Blessed are the poor in spirit: for theirs is the kingdom of heaven" (Matt. 5:3).

poverty, cure for—When love has begun its silent pulsations at one's center of consciousness, one cannot remain in want or poverty. From the invisible currents of the inner ether, love will draw to any man all that belongs to him, and all belongs to him that is required to make him happy and contented.

power—Man's innate control over his thoughts and

feelings. A quickening from on high must precede his realization of dominion. "Ye shall receive power, when the Holy Spirit is come upon you" (Acts 1:8). God is All-Power, thus all things are possible with Him.

The mind and the body of man have power to transform energy from one plane of consciousness to another. This is the power and dominion implanted in man from the beginning. The climax of man's power and dominion is set forth in the resurrection and ascension of the type man, Jesus.

In mind, power is increased through exalted ideas. These show us the relation between the world without and the mind within, and we find that they are parallel. Whatever you see in the external, you may be assured has its parallel in mind.

The same law is operating in the spiritual realm and the material realm under different masks of manifestation. The one thing to understand is that whatever we see without is controlled by something within. This law, once revealed to the mind, clears up the whole creation, and shows how God works.

Man is the power of God in action. To man is given the highest power in the universe, the conscious power of thought. There is a universal, creative force that urges man forward to the recognition of the creative power of his individual thought. This thought is elemental, and all its attributes come under the dominion of man. When he co-operates with Principle, man sits on the throne of his authority and the elemental force is subject to him.

Spiritual power is omnipresent. It is released in our body by spiritualizing our consciousness. This divine energy will surge through us as we erase negative thoughts from consciousness and become one with God-Mind.

powers, man's twelve—Faith, wisdom, love, life, power, strength, imagination, understanding, will, law of order, zeal, renunciation.

practical Christianity—The teachings of Jesus practically applied in one's daily life.

praise—The quality of mind that eulogizes the good; one of the avenues through which spirituality expresses.

The purpose of praise is to awaken in ourselves a higher realization of the omnipresence and power of God. Prayer and praise change man, not God. The mental attitude that praise sets up stimulates, quickens, whirls into action, and finally establishes in character the ideals of which they are the vehicle.

Through an inherent law of mind action we increase whatever we praise. The whole creation responds to praise, and is glad. Animals and children quickly respond to praise. One can praise a weak body into strength, a fearful heart into peace and trust, shattered nerves into poise and power, a failing business into prosperity and success, want and insufficiency into supply and support.

We make practical application of the law of praise by giving thanks always for all things, recognizing that "to them that love God all things work together for good" (Rom. 8:28).

prayer—Communion between God and man. This communion takes place in the innermost part of man's being. It is the only way to cleanse and perfect the consciousness and thus permanently heal the body.

Prayer is the most highly accelerated mind action known. It steps up mental action until man's consciousness synchronizes with the Christ Mind. It is the language of spirituality; when developed it makes man master in the realm of creative ideas.

Prayer is more than supplication. It is an affirmation of Truth that eternally exists, but which has not yet come into consciousness. It comes into consciousness not by supplication but by affirmation.

Do not supplicate or beg God to give you what you need, but get still and think about the inexhaustible resources of infinite Mind, its presence in all its fullness, and its constant readiness to manifest itself for you when its laws are complied with. This is what Jesus meant when He said, "Seek ye first his kingdom, and his righteousness; and all these things shall be added unto you" (Matt. 6:33).

It is necessary to pray believing that we have received because God is all that we desire. The good always exists in Divine Mind as ideas, and we bring it into manifestation through the prayer of faith, affirmation, praise, and acknowledgment.

All through the Scriptures, the different attitudes of mind necessary in prayer are pointed out. We are told to be instant in prayer, to pray with the Spirit, to pray in understanding. We have thought that prayer was something we could go to, in any way, at any time. But we have learned that to get results, we must pray with persistence and understanding, and with faith. This practice establishes a consciousness where doubt cannot enter. Jesus was in this consciousness. Is it possible for the ordinary man? Yes. But he must watch and pray. He must not only pray; he must watch also.

These are the seven necessary conditions for true prayer:

1. God should be recognized as Father.

2. Oneness with God should be acknowledged.

3. Prayer must be made within, in "the secret place" (Psalms 91).

4. The door must be closed on all thoughts and interests of the outer world.

5. The one who prays must believe that he has received.

6. The kingdom of God must be desired above all things, and sought first.

7. The mind must let go of every unforgiving thought.

prayer, chamber of—"Enter into thine inner chamber

and . . . shut thy door" (Matt. 6:6). The inner chamber is the "secret place of the Most High" (Psalms 91:1). It is the very depths of a man's consciousness. To enter it is to turn the attention from the without to the within. To "shut thy door" is to still the senses and close the mind against every disturbing exterior thought.

prayer, intercessory—The 17th chapter of John is known as the intercessory prayer. In this chapter Jesus first prayed for Himself, then for His apostles, and then for all who would accept salvation through Him, which prayer is extended to all generations.

"And now, Father, glorify thou me with thine own self with the glory which I had with thee before the world was. I manifested thy name unto the men whom thou gavest me out of the world" (John 17:5, 6). "I pray for them: I pray not for the world, but for those whom thou hast given me" (John 17:9). "Neither for these only do I pray, but for them also that believe on me" (John 17:20).

prayer for health—This prayer is the one most quickly answered, because natural laws that create and sustain the body are really divine laws. When man silently asks for the intervention of Spirit in restoring health, he is calling into increased activity the natural forces of the body. Through prayer the mind is renewed and the body transformed.

predestination—"The preordination of men to everlasting happiness or misery" (Webster). Since man is created in the image and after the likeness of God, he is predestined to bring the perfect pattern into expression. "I am God Almighty; walk before me, and be thou perfect" (Gen. 17:1).

The belief that God makes men do certain things cannot be true in a single instance, because, if it were, man would not be a free agent. If God interfered with man's will in some things, it would follow that He could interfere in any and all things. Logic and observation clearly reveal the freedom of man in everything. He was given freedom of thought, and must work out his own salvation.

It is well to use daily an affirmation such as this in the name of Jesus Christ: *I am the son of God, and the Spirit of the Most High dwells in me. I am the lord of my mind, and express only that which is constructive and upbuilding. I am predestined to be the perfect expression of my Father, and the fullness of all good is mine.*

predictions—The law of mind action will bring to pass what man believes in and expects. If he has faith in what he has been told by mediums and fortunetellers, he brings it to pass himself by his faith.

preparation, the—(John 19:31). Refers to the observances preliminary to the celebration of the Jewish Sabbath, or to the festival the day before the Sabbath. Among the Jews there was a law to the effect that a lifeless body should not remain on the cross on the Sabbath, as this was a day set aside for rest and freedom from all troubled or contentious thoughts.

presence of God—The awareness of Spirit within one's own being. It manifests as increased life, peace, love, and a deep sense of spiritual joy. (see *abiding Presence*)

presents—The presents that the Wise Men brought are symbolical of the inner resources open to the Christ child. They may be from the stored-up good deeds and thoughts of previous incarnations that the wisdom within carefully guards and gives to a man as an inheritance.

pride, spiritual—A form of personal vanity over spiritual achievement; a proud personal spirit; a "holier than thou" attitude.

"Blessed are the poor in [personal] spirit: for theirs is the kingdom of heaven" (Matt. 5:3).

priests—Metaphysically, ideas of priestly authority and the religious guidance of the intellect. The "priests and

Levites" represent our so-called natural religious tendencies. These officiate in the rites and ceremonies of the tent,
or tabernacle, and when the more permanent structure
(temple) is built, they bring up all the "holy vessels"
from the tent or tabernacle.

primary law and secondary law—Primary law is the
one law of God. Secondary law is the law of diet, of
economics, of medicine, and many other secondary things.
A true metaphysician always looks to the law of God.

prince of Peace—Jesus is the Prince of Peace. When
asking the Father for that which belongs to the Son under
the divine law, man should assume the power and dignity
of the Prince of Peace. He should not crawl and cringe
before an imaginary king on a throne but rather feel that
he is the image of an invisible Being who created him to
represent His mightiness as well as His loving-kindness.
We should affirm with conviction those mighty words of
Jesus: "All authority hath been given unto me in heaven
and on earth" (Matt. 28:18).

Principle—Fundamental Truth. Divine Principle is
fundamental Truth in a universal sense, or as pertaining to
God, the Divine. It is the underlying plan by which Spirit
(God) moves in expressing itself; the oversoul of this
planet which works its way into expression through Jesus.

God immanent in the universe is the great underlying
cause of all manifestation; the source from which form
proceeds. Although Principle is formless, it is that by which
all form is produced.

Principle is the I AM of every man. As the principle
of music moves through tones, so does the principle of
mind move through ideas. A word is a spoken thought, or
idea. Therefore, God as creative Mind, moves through the
expressed thought of Divine Mind, referred to in Scripture
as the Word of God.

progress, spiritual—Growth in the conception and expression of spiritual ideas.

Promised Land—Metaphysically, a realization of divine substance. It is the foundation of the substratum of the new body in Christ. It is not a dream that man is to possess a body of immortality.

When there wells up in a man a great desire to be free from the bondage of ignorance and the animal propensities, his journey to the Promised Land begins.

promises, God's—Free will gives to man the privilege to accept or reject the promises of God. If he rejects them there is no way for them to be fulfilled in him.

No one who holds back part of the price can find the way into the kingdom. The works of the flesh must be entirely overcome. Every flesh desire must be put away so that the pure and holy desires of the Christ man may be given expression. All the life substance must be conserved, spiritualized, and used in making the body whole and perfect like the body of the Lord Jesus Christ.

prophet—One who receives the inspiration of Spirit, understands spiritual law, and imparts it to others. The prophets of old seemed to stand between God and the people; it was through them that the people received divine guidance.

Metaphysically, the prophet is that in us which discerns the working of the law. Transgressed law brings its own punishment, and it is the prophet of the Lord that sees its outworking in our life. It is the prophet in us that often warns and keeps us from transgressing the law, because we discern what the result will be.

prophets, false—Deceptive thoughts that have been built up by error; selfish desires. False prophets are the representations of deceptive religious thoughts. They seem innocent and harmless like sheep, but are in reality selfish and dangerous. "Beware of false prophets, who come to you in sheep's clothing, but inwardly are ravening wolves" (Matt: 7:15).

proselyte—Metaphysically, one who has turned away

from the old, set, religious forms and ceremonies, and realizes Truth for himself.

proselyting—The act of one endeavoring to convert another to his way of thinking. This is not in accord with divine law. The Spirit of truth within is man's one and only guide.

No one has the right to dictate what another shall do. However, we do teach principles boldly without regard to whether mortal man accepts or rejects. It is ours to give forth the Truth; the responsibility of acceptance rests with those who hear. If the higher self hears the Word and the lower self resists and rebels, that is a matter for the individual to work out according to his own choice and faith.

prosperity—The consciousness of God as the abundant, everywhere present resource, unfailing, ready for all who open themselves to it through faith. "They that seek Jehovah shall not want any good thing" (Psalms 34:10).

Prosperity is based on the conscious possession of the idea of God's abundance back of all things. Things come and go, but the idea of abundance endures. Things appear at its command. Jesus had no visible possessions, but He could supply thousands of persons with food through praising and giving thanks to the invisible Spirit of plenty.

The difference between spiritual prosperity and material prosperity is that spiritual prosperity is founded on understanding of the inexhaustible, omnipresent substance of Spirit as the source of supply; the material belief is that the possession of things constitutes prosperity.

"Lay not up for yourselves treasures upon the earth . . but lay up for yourselves treasures in heaven" (Matt. 6:19-20).

In demonstrating prosperity, you should praise and give thanks for every little evidence of financial improvement. Be confident of the immediate co-operation of God's Spirit with you in bringing to pass that for which you have given thanks. The divine resource never fails. God is the omnipresent, unfailing resource for all who trust Him and who make all their thoughts chord with Divine Mind. God is your prosperity. Stamp this thought daily on your mind and you will reap financial success.

Giving in the right mental attitude creates prosperity. Giving with the fear of lack leads to poverty. Giving with the thought of a large resource opens the way for a large income. "Give, and it shall be given unto you; good measure, pressed down, shaken together, running over" (Luke 6:38).

psalm—The Truth of God spoken in poetry or music; a hymn of praise or joy; spiritual aspiration of the soul. "Is any cheerful? let him sing praise" (James 5:13).

psyche—A word prominent in Greek mythology, meaning "the soul." Psyche may be thought of as man in his many earthly experiences, in his failures and his successes.

psychic—Pertaining to mental powers not common to ordinary man; mental powers outreaching the scope of the physical man, but not yet quickened to the standard of Spirit.

Man has a body in the ether that is the counterpart of the physical. It is through this psychic body that he has sensations in the physical. It is possible to think of the psychic body and cultivate its sensations until it appears as real as the physical. Many persons have done this until they have formed a psychic world consciousness and are often unable to separate it from the physical. To them the realm of thought forms is the finality of creation instead of the mental pictures of that which is about to appear.

The first step of a Truth student in handling the psychic forces of consciousness is the same as that in handling any other, and that is to realize that God is the one and only power; to declare with Byron: "There is no god but God!—to prayer—lo! God is great!"

Next make conscious contact with this all-powerful God-Mind and realize that every phase of the mind, every thought is brought into the captivity of the Christ, and that through your I AM power and dominion you are master over every situation.

psychoanalysis—Analysis of the subconscious mind. The followers of Jesus go one step farther in mind therapy than the psychoanalyst; they incorporate Spirit with soul and make Spirit the primal source and sustainer of both soul and body. "It is the spirit that giveth life" (John 6:63).

psychology and religion—Thought control is imperative, and there is urgent need of teachers on both the mental and spiritual plane of consciousness if the race is to go forward in development. To this end there needs to be more co-operation between these two schools, because they complement each other. Religion becomes practical and effective in everyday life when it incorporates psychology as part of its litany. Without religion psychology is weak in its fundamentals, and without psychology religion fails to give proper attention to the outlet of its ideals. The fact is that religion, comprehended in its fullness, includes psychology. Jesus was a profound psychologist.

The carping critic cries, "Your religion is psychology instead of Christianity." Our answer is that the new Christianity includes an understanding of psychology and does not stop with an analysis of the mind but goes on to the highest phase of mind's possibilities, unity with Spirit.

punishment—Man does not receive punishment from an outside force. Man punishes himself by holding false thoughts. He escapes from punishment as soon as he aligns his thought with that of God.

pure in heart—The "pure in heart" are those who are completely free from all anxiety, resentment, selfishness, lust, and every other form of antichrist thought and feeling. "Blessed are the pure in heart: for they shall see God" (Matt. 5:8).

purity of the Christ Mind—The deep purity and mighty strength of the Christ Mind are made manifest in men as they develop spiritually. Instead of consciously and unconsciously tempting one another in sense ways, these qualities in each will incite in the other holy aspirations to fulfill the law of righteousness. "And every one that hath this hope *set* on him purifieth himself, even as he [the Father] is pure" (I John 3:3).

purification of blood—If your lung capacity is not equal to the purification of your blood, increase it by declaring the law of active life. Anemic blood may be made vigorous and virile by daily centering the attention in the lungs and affirming them to be spiritual, and under the perpetual inflow of new life and the outflow of old life the lungs will do your will.

Q

quality, spiritual—That which is characteristic of one's spiritual nature. High spiritual qualities are established in man's body consciousness through prayer and profound spiritual aspiration.

quickening, spiritual—An inflow of divine vitality into the body, which follows the affirmation of Truth. To quicken is to make alive. The quickening of the Spirit in the mortal body makes it eternal and incorruptible, not subject to death and corruption.

Spiritual quickening is a waking up of the whole man to the full consciousness of what he is in the sight of God. The sense man is only half-awake, going about in a dream and thinking it is real life. The word of God is quick, and when it enters into a man he stands upright on his feet, his divine understanding, and he knows and sees himself as he is. He is wide awake, alert, quick, and powerful.

"But if the Spirit of him that raised up Jesus from the dead dwelleth in you, he that raised up Christ Jesus from the dead shall give life also to your mortal bodies through his Spirit that dwelleth in you" (Rom. 8:11).

quietness—When the mind is stilled, when all the clamor of the external world is silenced, one experiences the quietness of God. "In returning and rest shall ye be saved; in quietness and in confidence shall be your strength" (Isa. 30:15).

R

race consciousness—The human race has formed laws of physical birth and death, laws of sickness and physical inability, laws making food the source of bodily existence, laws of mind that recognize no other source of existence except the physical. The sum total of these laws forms a race consciousness separate from and independent of creative Mind. When creative Mind sought to help men spiritually, the mind of the flesh opposed it and made every effort to solve its problems in its own way. The great need of the human family is mind control. Jesus showed us that mastery is attained through realization of the power of Spirit.

race errors—Erroneous race thoughts that bind mankind to sin, disease, poverty, war, calamity, and death.

race mind—Totality of beliefs, thoughts, memories, feelings, and experiences of the race. Man has built into the race mind a consciousness of corruptible flesh instead of the inherent incorruptible substance of God-Mind.

radiation—An extension of consciousness. Jesus' soul radiation or aura was so powerful that it perpetually stimulates to greater achievement, and thrills with new life all who enter its sphere of influence. (see *aura*)

rain—Metaphysically, an outpouring of Spirit that constantly refreshes and enriches man's developing thoughts. The descent of potential ideas into substance. The rain that "watereth the earth" represents the love of God, which comes into mind when summoned and needed.

raising of Lazarus—The restoration in consciousness of the idea of youth, which is asleep in the subconsciousness.

rats—Represent destructive, undermining, gnawing thoughts.

raven, going forth of a—The raven's going forth represents the reaching out of the thought from within to connect with the outer world. There is an individual consciousness, which is the ark, and a universal consciousness, which is the heavens and the earth.

rays—All mental action radiates rays of light. Clairvoyants and psychics have long claimed that they can see these rays surrounding not only human beings, but animals, plants, and even stones. Their claims have been considered chimerical until in the last few years, when science found that it can measure the force of these invisible rays. The character of the thoughts colors the emanations of these rays. If the thoughts pertain to the things of sense, the rays are dark and weak; if the affectional and intellectual nature is active, they become highly colored and forceful. When the mind is exalted in prayer, a dazzling light radiates from all parts of the body, but especially from the head.

rays, healing—Spiritual rays superior to the ultraviolet rays that come from the sun. They heal both mind and body.

reality—That which is abiding, eternal, and unchangeable, the same "yesterday and to-day, *yea* and for ever" (Heb. 13:8). The basic principles of mathematics and music are real, because they are not subject to change. A wrong application of their principles may produce discord, but the principles are not disturbed. God is the one harmonious Principle underlying all being and the reality out of which all that is eternal comes.

All causes are in mind. Error thoughts produce the mental and physical inharmonies called disease. These effects are not enduring and eternal. Error can be erased from the mind and be made to disappear from the body.

realization—The deep inner conviction and assurance of the fulfillment of an ideal. It means at-one-ment, completion, perfection, wholeness, repose, resting in God. It is the dawning of Truth in the consciousness. When realization takes place, one abides in the light of God-Mind. It is the inner conviction that prayer has been answered, although there is as yet no outer manifestation.

The supreme realization is unity with God-Mind, complete oneness with the Christ consciousness. This highest realization is taking place more widely today among men than at any time in all history. Jesus fully attained this supreme realization.

realm, spiritual—The higher realm of consciousness built in accordance with the Christ ideal. The realm of Spirit is wherever God is working to express Himself. When man as principle becomes the perfect image and likeness of God, no other realm will appear to have being.

rebellion—Open defiance and resistance to an authority to which one owes allegiance. One rebels because he believes he is not being rightly governed, his conditions are not satisfactory. Man has been taught that God brought on him sickness, poverty, inharmony, and that these conditions are the will of God. While he recognizes that God is supreme ruler and governor of all things, man rebels at such conditions being imposed on him. As soon as a man comes into the understanding that his own thoughts and words are the cause of the conditions in his life, he no longer rebels and blames God. He uses his creative thought power, he sets the Word into right activity, and good comes into his life.

receiving— (see *giving*)

receptivity, spiritual—The attitude of mind that awaits the higher way as a little child awaits the helping hand of a parent. It is not the arbitrary disciplinarian, but the loving, tender, understanding heart that in visible life lightens the intricate problems that perplex the mind. When one who is receptive and obedient gives himself unreservedly to Spirit and receives without antagonism its guidance, he is delighted with the possibilities that are disclosed to him in caring for his physical and spiritual needs. He then begins to realize what Jesus meant when He said, "If any man would come after me, let him deny himself, and take up his cross, and follow me" (Matt. 16:24).

recompense—The satisfaction and uplift that one feels after a realization of Truth.

re-creation—The process of redemption; a gradual transformation that takes place as man pays the price, gives up self, and allows Spirit to work in mind and body.

redemption—The process by which the life and substance of man's lesser self are brought to conform to the standards of his spiritual self. The body is redeemed from destruction by attaining spiritual consciousness on earth. "For this corruptible must put on incorruption" (I Cor. 15:53).

regeneration—A change in which abundant spiritual life, even eternal life, is incorporated into the body. The transformation that takes place through bringing all the forces of mind and body to the support of the Christ ideal. The unification of Spirit, soul, and body in spiritual oneness.

Regeneration begins its work in the conscious mind and completes it in the subconsciousness. The first step is cleansing or denial in which all error thoughts are renounced. This includes forgiveness for sins committed and a general clearing of the whole consciousness. After the way has been prepared, the second step takes place. This is the outpouring of the Holy Spirit.

reincarnation—When a soul leaves the body, it rests for a season. Then innate desire for material expression asserts itself, and the ego seeks the primal cell and builds another body. This is reincarnation. Reincarnation will continue until the ego awakens to the Christ Mind and through it builds an imperishable body.

The law of Being is broken by sin and death. Resurrection or regeneration in this body here and now—not reincarnation—is the aim of overcomers. Reincarnation is the result of man's use of the great forces of Mind, enabling an ego or soul that has been separated from the vehicle of expression (the body) again to attract to it the necessary substance to reconstruct the body-consciousness and to have another opportunity for the demonstration of the Truth of Being, but reincarnation is not a part of the divine plan and does not lift man out of mortal limitations. It is not an aid to spiritual growth, but merely a makeshift until full Truth is discerned.

relaxation—A letting go of tenseness in mind and body. Abatement of strain. Loosening the tight mental grip we have on ourselves in order that the healing Christ life may flow freely through our being. "Come unto me . . . and I will give you rest" (Matt. 11:28).

religion—A systematic exposition on the awareness of a deity who is the supreme ruler of heaven and earth; that which arouses reverence and love for a supreme being. There is a wide range of religious experience between the blindly groping faith that caused men to pass their children through the fire as sacrifice to their deities, and the divine consciousness of Jesus, who submitted His body to the purifying fire of the Spirit and came forth alive with a life that never dies.

In the study of things pertaining to religion we should keep in mind the three activities of consciousness: spiritual, psychical, and physical. The spiritual is the realm of absolute principles; the psychical is the realm of thought images; the physical is the realm of manifestation. The well-balanced, thoroughly developed man, of which Jesus is the type, comprehends and consciously adjusts his spirit, soul, and body as a whole, and thereby fulfills the law of his being. Those who are on the way to this attainment have various experiences, which are symbolically set forth in the Scriptures.

renunciation—A letting go of old thoughts in order that new thoughts may find place in consciousness. A healthy state of mind is attained when the thinker willingly lets go the old thoughts and takes on the new. This is illustrated by the inlet and outlet of a pool of water. The center of renunciation, sometimes called elimination, in the lower part of the abdomen, carries forward the work of elimination of error thoughts from the mind and waste from the body.

repentance—A turning from a belief in sin and error to a belief in God and righteousness; a reversal of mind and heart in the direction of the All-Good. When we repent, we break with mortal thought and ascend into a spiritual thought realm, the kingdom of God.

The Greek word *metanoia* is translated "repentance," which has been interpreted to mean an admission to God of sorrow for past sin and a resolve to be good in the future. The field of action for that which has been assumed to be goodness in the sight of God has nearly always been in conduct.

There is always hope for the repentant sinner. A repentant state of mind is an exceedingly good state for one who has been on the error side. If you find yourself suffering the result of transgressed law, begin at once a righteous repentance. As soon as you repent and recognize that the way of Spirit is the way of pleasantness, your sins are forgiven you, and you are made whole and well.

repetitions, vain—When we rehearse affirmations just because they are given to us to hold, with no thought of their inner reality, or if we are in a doubtful state of mind, they become "vain repetitions." It is true that a declaration of Truth may not at first repeating find lodgment in consciousness and that we may repeat it over and over before it becomes a living word, but the attitude of mind as we go through this process is the seed that bears fruit, the assurance of the harvest. Nothing outside of man can affect him when he is in contact with his inner spiritual source.

resistance—The greatest disintegrating element in the human consciousness is resistance. Beware of every form of fighting, and of all thoughts of a destructive character. Thoughts build or destroy, and they will work in your mind and body in an adverse way and tear down the good you desire to build up if you do not form them with care.

A mental state of resistance indicates an unyielding personal will. Evil has no power except that which man gives it by his thought. Resisting evil is a way of affirming its power. A positive, fearless attitude in facing the appearance of evil overcomes it, and this attitude comes from the understanding that evil has no power.

restitution—The resurrection of man to the divine image and likeness in mind and body and to the dominion that has been his from the beginning. The restitution work also includes the earth, which is to be redeemed from the curse that fell on it through sin. It is to blossom and bring forth and be a paradise, a fitting home for redeemed man.

restlessness—The unsatisfied longing of a man for God. Restlessness cannot be satisfied by change of climate or environment or by travel or by any other outward change. Only by a man's finding his center in God can restlessness and discontent be satisfied.

"For he satisfieth the longing soul,
And the hungry soul he filleth with good"
(Psalms 107:9).

restorative power of nature—The term given by doctors to the Spirit of health, which is always right at hand awaiting opportunity to enter in to make whole and to harmonize all discord in the body.

resurrection—The restoring of mind and body to their original, undying state. This is accomplished by the realization that God is Spirit and that God created man with power like that which He Himself possesses. When man realizes this, his mind and body automatically become immortal. "If the Spirit of him that raised up Jesus from the dead dwelleth in you, he that raised up Christ Jesus from the dead shall give life also to your mortal bodies through his Spirit that dwelleth in you" (Rom. 8:11). The word *resurrection* also suggests that there has been a falling short of the divine standard; therefore, the necessity of being restored and revived. Through resurrection man becomes an inhabitant here and now of "a new heaven and a new earth" (Rev. 21:1).

Jesus was raised from the dead. He overcame death in the body. "For since by man *came* death, by man *came* also the resurrection of the dead." Physical death is not necessary. "We all shall not sleep, but we shall all be changed" (I Cor. 15:21, 51).

The power of the resurrection is the Christ. "I am the resurrection, and the life" (John 11:25). This resurrection is not of the future, "but hath now been manifested by . . . our Saviour Christ Jesus, who abolished death, and brought life and immortality to light" (II Tim. 1:10).

Christ, absolute Principle, the God-idea man, is the true resurrecting power and life in each of us here and now. Jesus resurrected His body through the spiritual I AM dwelling in Him.

The resurrection takes place in us every time we rise to Jesus' realization of the perpetual indwelling life that is connecting us with the Father. A new flood of life comes to all who open their minds and their bodies to the living word of God.

revelation—An unveiling, a disclosure of Truth, making known that which is hidden. The revelation of Christ to all men is the ultimate revelation.

Divine revelation is much more common than is understood. The Spirit of truth is revealing the hidden wisdom to thousands on every hand. Poets and writers of Truth are being inspired of the Most High. Quiet citizens in every walk of life are the recipients of the divine word. Every man who has earnestly asked for divine guidance, or who has earnestly desired to do right in the sight of God and man, is being taught by the Holy Spirit.

reverence—The attitude of reverence is an important feature in developing the Christ consciousness. Without it the mind loses a certain necessary connection with Spirit and lacks that central poise of faith that gives a religious tenor to the process.

rich young man—(Mark 10:17-27). Personality; the state of consciousness in man that lays hold of the world of form, seeking satisfaction in personal possessions and in fulfilling the letter of the law.

righteousness—A state of harmony established in consciousness through the right use of God-given attributes. It leads directly to eternal life. Truth working in consciousness brings forth the perfect salvation of the whole man— Spirit, soul, and body—and righteousness (right relation) is expressed in all his affairs.

right side—The "right side" (John 21:6) is always on the side of Truth, the side of power. Whenever you, the master, are there, the nets are filled with ideas, because you are in touch with the infinite storehouse of wisdom.

rites—The rites and ceremonies of the priests in the tabernacle or temple represent the action of spiritual forces in developing the body. The great object of man's existence in planetary consciousness is to build a body after the

ideals given by the Lord. The physical body is the tabernacle or temporary structure in and through which the enduring body is formed, and regeneration is a combination
of chemical, mental, and spiritual processes.

river of life—The source of the natural healing impulse
that constantly reconstructs the organism. When a man in
faith makes intimate connection between his mind and the
Father's, he enters into the river of life. And he has the
ability to take others with him into the waters that cleanse,
purify, and vitalize.

rod—Metaphysically, the power of the I AM in spiritual consciousness; I AM mastery and dominion.

roll, burning of—The burning of the roll (Jer. 36th
chapter) represents a denial by the spiritual thought working in consciousness. To go forward to more advanced
demonstrations, we must give up the present ruling ideas.

When we reach a point in our ongoing where there is
necessity of greater spirituality, our own meditations reveal
to us that the way is through reforming our methods of
thought and life. This is the intuitive perception of the
progressive trend of all things, which is symbolized in the
burning of the "roll" by the king. The lesson is that we
shall read out of the "roll" of the higher wisdom the new
revelations of Truth that are being constantly presented to
us and be open and receptive to divine evolution.

room, upper—The storehouse of ideas. The I AM
center is in the crown of the head and dispenses the substance and life and intelligence of Spirit.

rulership—In personal rulership the great ones exercise
authority; he who rules lords it over his subjects. In spiritual rulership he who serves best is greatest and is ruler
through true merit. (see Matt. 20:25-28)

Jesus is the greatest ruler the world has ever known
because He served humanity best, even to overcoming
death itself; through His demonstration the way to eternal
life was opened to humanity.

S

sabachthani—In *sabachthani* we find the root idea of loosening, setting free; letting alone and forsaking are secondary developments. The real root idea of the word expressed the cutting loose of bondage, or freeing from slavery.

On the cross Jesus cried, "Eli, Eli lama sabachthani?" that is, "My God, my God, why hast thou forsaken me?" (Matt. 27:46).

Metaphysically, *sabachthani* is the cry of the soul at the darkest hour of crucifixion. When the sensual is passing away it seems as though man were giving up his life, including every good. The sensual looms so large at this hour that, for the time being, it shuts God from the consciousness of the individual who is going through the experience. But God never forsakes His children; there can be no real separation from the divine, and a glorious resurrection into a greater degree of spiritual life than was ever realized before always follows each letting go of the old.

Sabbath—The true Sabbath is that state of spiritual attainment where man ceases from all personal effort and all belief in his own works, and rests in the consciousness that "the Father abiding in me doeth his works" (John 14:10). When we understand the true spirit of the Sabbath, we cease following prescribed rules laid down by a church and open our mind to God's rest and peace. We rest from outer work, cease daily occupation, and give ourselves up to meditation or the study of things spiritual.

The Sabbath is kept any time we enter into spiritual consciousness and rest from thoughts of temporal things. We let go of the external observance of days, because every day is a Sabbath on which we retire into Spirit and worship God.

sacrifice—A refining process that is constantly going on in consciousness; the renunciation of old beliefs that seem good for new ideas that are more of the nature of Christ.

salt of the earth—The thoughts in man that understand, love, and obey Truth as Jesus taught and demonstrated it.

salvation—The restitution of man to his spiritual birthright; regaining conscious possession of his God-given attributes. It comes as the result of redemption; the change from sin to righteousness. Salvation comes to man as a free gift from God. It embodies a knowledge of God that frees one from all limitations and points the way by which mind and body may be lifted up to the spiritual place of consciousness.

The belief that Jesus in an outer way atoned for our sins is not salvation. Salvation is based solely on an inner overcoming, a change in consciousness. It is a cleansing of the mind, through Christ, from thoughts of evil.

sanctification—The putting on of the nature of God and rising to the plane of dominion that gives man peace and satisfaction; the purity and holiness of the Christ consciousness. "This is the will of God, *even* your sanctification" (I Thess. 4:3).

sanctuary of the soul—The secret place within man's being where he has a rendezvous with God.

Satan—The Adversary, the great universal negative whose power is derived from the unlawful expression of man's own being. The serpent as "Satan" is sensation suggesting indulgence in pleasures beyond the law fixed by creative Mind.

Saviour—The Christ Mind is our Saviour. Through the Christ Mind we find salvation from poverty, sickness, sin, and death.

sayings of Jesus—To keep the sayings of Jesus is to

take the spiritual principles that He enunciated and square our own life by them, that is, use them as a working basis in all the life processes.

science, spiritual—Science is the systematic and orderly arrangement of knowledge. Spiritual science, which is the orderly arrangement of the truths of Being, does not always conform to intellectual standards, but it is still scientific. Spiritual science treats of absolute ideas, while mental science treats of limited thoughts.

scribes—Scribes represent the thoughts that come to us from the outer world; Spirit inspires us from within. When Spirit speaks, no person can be quoted as authority—the Truth itself is authority, and it bows to no human exponent.

"For he taught them as having authority, and not as the scribes" (Mark 1:22).

Scriptures—Although the Holy Scriptures are almost universally considered to be the printed Bible only, the real Scriptures are the book of life within our own consciousness. The written word, however, is meant as a clue to a more vital part of the Scriptures than appears, since there is both a literal and a spiritual significance to them.

The Scriptures are not like other books. They have an enduring life, because of the spiritual quality given them by the writers. They are a profitable source of instruction in righteousness, as they set forth the principle, or law, of eternal life.

The Scriptures contain in symbol a most wonderful description of the creative action of Divine Mind, and one who studies the Bible merely as a historical record or as a guide to morals fails to sound the depths of these ancient writings.

Truth students recognize that Bible history is something more than history. For example, they see in the journey of the Israelites to the Promised Land, a picture of man's

progress from sense consciousness to spiritual consciousness.

season of fruits—Bringing forth of the various powers
of consciousness.

second coming—The second coming is the result of
building the principles of Being into the soul of man,
where they begin to express through him.

The events in the life of Jesus of Nazareth represent
certain stages of spiritual growth in natural man. Jesus
was the incarnation of the Son of God, and was the great
Example, the Way-Shower, and manifested the Mind of
God. If we are to attain full sonship we must follow His
example. The second coming is right upon us. The Spirit
of the Lord Jesus is here right now, and has been ever since
He gave His spiritual body and blood to the race consciousness.

"secret place of the Most High"—(see *inner chamber*)

sects—In the spiritual interpretation of fundamental
principles that underly the Scriptures, there are no sects, no
differences among Truth students. But when the Bible is
read according to the letter instead of the spirit, each reader
views it from his own personal standpoint. This gives rise
to a variety of opinions. Many a person who has what he
considers the right viewpoint, tries to gain a following and
convert others to his ideas, and in this way sects have
been formed.

seed—The creative idea inherent in the Word. Its
nature is inherited from its parent source, God. The "seed,"
that is, "the word of God," is the real man—not the external thinking personality that has consciousness of separation, but the internal Spirit center. The seed is a generative
center through which intelligence manipulates substance
and produces form. In itself it is powerless to produce anything, but it is the avenue through which interior forces
manifest in the outer. Man draws on the universal forces

within and without, just as the tree draws on the invisible Spirit and earth, air, and water.

The illustration of the mustard seed is used to show the capacity of the apparently small thought of Truth to develop in consciousness until it becomes the abiding place of a higher range of thoughts (birds of the air).

"**seek the things that are above**"—(Col: 3:1). Seek spirituality, instead of materiality. Seek to unfold the Christ Mind and to abide in spiritual consciousness. This leads into the path of peace, joy, and abundance of all good.

selah—Tranquil, secure, at rest, silence, pause, quiet. Selah is that state of mind in which we relax from affirming Truth and wait on God in the stillness. Then the Holy Spirit may reveal more of its inspirations to us and may establish us more firmly in divine harmony and good.

self-control—The capacity to direct one's behavior in right ways.

One who tries to establish self-control through will power and suppression never accomplishes permanent results. Self-control is accomplished when all the forces of man come in touch with the divine will and understanding.

self—Christ, the divine idea, is the true self of every man. Adam, the natural man, is the incomplete self. The fulfillment of self is accomplished as man puts on the Christ.

selfishness—Overconcern for one's own interests or comfort and disregard for the welfare of others. Selfishness leads to strife, followed by anger and hate. These emotions generate thought currents that burn up the body cells in somewhat the way a live wire sears flesh. Selfishness is often the cause of unhappiness.

self-love—Care for one's own happiness and well-being. This care is entirely compatible with justice, generosity, and love for others.

"Thou shalt love the Lord thy God with all thy heart,

and with all thy soul, and with all thy strength, and with all thy mind; and thy neighbor as thyself" (Luke 10:27).

selling one's birthright—When one denies his true inheritance as a son of God, in thought, word, or deed, he is to that extent selling his birthright.

sensation—A state of excited interest or feeling derived from stimulation of the sense organs. Spirituality, lifts up this divine creation and restores it to its pristine beauty. Through cultivation of the spiritual nature, sensation is crowned with purity, and the son of man becomes aware of God's presence in his body as life, power, love, and joy.

sense consciousness—A mental state formed from believing in and acting through the senses. It is the serpent consciousness, deluded with sensation.

Judgments based on outer appearances—the senses—produce discordant thoughts, jealousies, and a host of limiting beliefs.

senses, how to develop the—By declaring our senses to be spiritual and by speaking the increasing word of the I AM to every one of them, we multiply their capacities and give them a sustaining vigor and vitality. This is done through the simple word of the I AM, backed up by the realization of its spiritual power.

separation from God—Man, being the offspring of God, has the power to create. He has used his privilege and created a realm of error thought, which separates him in consciousness from the Father.

separation of religion and state—Some statesmen and politicians urge the separation of religion and state because they do not understand the true character or mission of religion. The clergy are responsible for this misconception; they emphasize the saving of the soul, that it may be prepared to dwell happily in heaven after death. This teaching removes religion from its true field of work, which is making people better and happier here and now. As a result of this teaching that the greater rewards of religion will come after death, Christianity has been robbed of the major part of its power as a harmonizer of worldly affairs. Jesus did not promise rewards after death, but on the contrary, emphasized service in this world as the supreme thing. Mortal man thinks leadership is evidence of greatness, but Jesus taught that greatness is attained through service.

seraphim—Ideas of purity; the cleansing power of exalted ideas.

serpent—Sense consciousness or the desire of unspiritualized man for sensation. He seeks satisfaction through the appetite. By listening to the serpent of sense, man falls to his lowest estate.

sheep—Harmless and innocent animals; they represent the natural life that flows into man's consciousness from Spirit. It is pure, innocent, guileless.

The separation of goats from sheep is a mental process wherein the good, obedient, and profitable thoughts (sheep) are retained (placed on the right hand). The stubborn, selfish, useless thoughts (goats) are put away (placed on the left hand).

Sheba—The Queen of Sheba indicates the ruling intelligence of the whole consciousness pertaining to the part of being that has to do with nature.

shepherds—The shepherds watching by night are the protecting entities of God that watch over us. They are the conservers and protectors. To affirm "Jehovah is my shepherd" is to acknowledge that God (Spirit) is the source of understanding and of all help.

seven—the number *seven* represents fullness in the world of phenomena; *seven* refers to the divine law of perfection for the divine-natural man.

seven golden candlesticks—Refers to the seven nerve centers in the organism that have been quickened, purified, and transmuted into spiritual intelligence.

seven stars—The sevenfold powers of man in intelligent action are represented by the seven stars.

shoes—Represent the words with which understanding (Truth) is clothed. When holy ground, or substance in its spiritual wholeness, is approached by man he must put off from his understanding all limited thoughts about the Absolute—he must put his shoes off his feet.

shortcomings—Mental transgressions, which must be mentally denied. Many persons refuse to deny their shortcomings. They hold that they are perfect in Divine Mind and that it is superfluous to deny that which has no existence. But they are still subject to the appetites and passions of mortality, and will continue to be until they are "born anew." The Pharisees refused to be baptized by John. They did not consider that they needed the repentance that He demanded. They thought they were good enough to take the high places in the kingdom of God because of their popularly accepted religious supremacy.

silence, the—A state of consciousness entered into for the purpose of putting man in touch with Divine Mind so that the soul may listen to the "still small voice" (I Kings 19:12).

When one goes into the silence he enters the "secret place of the Most High," the closet of prayer within. He closes the door and in the stillness of that meeting place he prays to God, he communes with God, and he meditates on Truth. Then he listens to what God has to say to him.

silver and gold—Symbolize love and wisdom.

sin—Missing the mark; that is, falling short of divine perfection. Sin is man's failure to express the attributes of Being—life, love, intelligence, wisdom, and the other God qualities.

Sin (error) is first in mind and is redeemed by a mental process, or by going into the silence. Error is brought into the light of Spirit and then transformed into a constructive force. "Be ye transformed by the renewing of your mind" (Rom. 12:2).

Through the Christ Mind, our sins (wrong thinking) are forgiven or pardoned (erased from consciousness). When we have cast all sin (error thought) out of our mind, our body will be so pure that it cannot come under any supposed law of death or corruption.

singing—Singing, praising, and thanksgiving are the great building impulses of man. Never repress the desire to give thanks through happy songs and words of praise.

Singing restores harmony to tense nerves because its vibrations stir them to action, thus making it possible for the ever-waiting, healing Spirit to get in. The organ of the human voice is located right between the thyroid glands, the accelerators of certain important body functions. To a greater or lesser degree every word one speaks vibrates the cells up and down the body, from front brain to abdomen.

single eye—The single eye sees only God (good) everywhere. This perfect vision heals all disease in mind, body, and affairs. "The lamp of the body is the eye: if therefore thine eye be single, thy whole body shall be full of light" (Matt. 6:22).

six days of creation—The six great ideal projections from Divine Mind, each more comprehensive than its predecessor. The climax is reached when that phase of Being called man appears, having dominion over the ideas that have gone before.

sleep—Sleep is a great harmonizer of discordant thoughts. It "knits up the ravell'd sleave of care." We do not know the deep mysteries of sleep or what goes on in the soul when the sense man is in repose. Those who go into the "deep silence" produce a state of consciousness analogous to sleep. All the outer thoughts are stilled, and the soul listens to the "still small voice." It may also see symbols, feel the inner forces, or catch divine ideas fresh from the Fountainhead. Those who are expert in concentrating the attention on inner planes of Being find that a great rest and peace comes to them. Upon emerging from one of these sweet periods of communion with the Lord, they feel as if they have had a night of refreshing sleep.

solar plexus—The vital center of the organism, through which the subconscious mind connects with the physical body. The solar plexus is a large nerve center lying back of the pit of the stomach, and it controls the activity of the stomach.

Solomon's Temple—With its inner and outer courts, it is a symbolical representation of man's body.

Son of God—The fullness of the perfect-man idea in Divine Mind, the Christ. The true spiritual self of every individual. The living Word; the Christ idea in the Mind of God.

The Son ever exists in God. Father and Son are one and are omnipresent in man and the universe. Jesus represents God's idea of man in expression (Son of man); Christ is that idea in the Absolute (Son of God). The Christ is the man that God created in His image and likeness, the perfect-idea man. He is the real self of all men.

Son of man—That in us which discerns the difference between Truth and error. When we get this understanding we are in a position to free our soul from sin and our body from disease, which is the effect of sin. The Son of man must be lifted up, and there is no way to do this except through prayer.

son, prodigal—The "two sons" of Luke 15:11 are the two departments of the soul, or consciousness. The son who stayed at home is the religious or moral nature; the son who went into the far country is the human phase of the soul, in which are the appetites and passions. Going into a "far country" is separating the consciousness from the parent Source.

The first step in complying with the law of return to

the Father's house is repentance and confession. Confession should be made to God. If we are truly repentant, the Father will forgive; He will have compassion, and the bounty of Divine Mind will be poured out on us.

When we make unity between the outer sense and the inner Spirit (the return of the prodigal son to the Father's house), there is great rejoicing; the outer is flooded with the vitality (robe), unending power is put into his hand (ring), and his understanding (feet) is strengthened. The "fatted calf" is the richness of strength always awaiting the needy soul. When all these relations have been established between the within and the without, there is rejoicing. The dead man of sense is made alive in the consciousness of Spirit—the lost is found.

song— (see *singing*)

sonship—Man, through Christ within, is God's son. Man reveals his sonship to himself and to others by claiming it; by declaring that he is not a son of mortality but a son of God; that the Spirit of God dwells within him and shines through him; that this Spirit is Christ, Son of God.

soul—Man's consciousness; the underlying idea back of any expression. In man, the soul is the many accumulated ideas back of his present expression. In its original and true sense, the soul of man is the expressed idea of man in Divine Mind.

Man is Spirit, soul, and body. Spirit is the I AM, the individuality. The body is soul expressing, and soul includes the conscious and subconscious minds. Soul makes the body, the body is the outer expression of the soul, and bodily health is in exact correspondence to the health of the soul.

soul development—The unfoldment of divine ideals in the soul, or consciousness of man, and the bringing of these ideals into expression in the body.

soul, duality of the—That phase of the soul named subconsciousness, which draws its life from both the earthly side of existence and the spiritual; it answers to both good and evil, light and darkness.

soul, food for the—The soul is fed by thought; the true soul food is the Word of God. The Word of God when properly appropriated makes the soul immortal.

source of all good—God is the source of all good. All good things flow to us from Him through love and grace. "All that is mine is thine" (Luke 15:31).

sowing—Every thought is a seed and brings forth after its kind. Every carnal thought, or thought of selfishness in any form, is seed sown to the flesh. It brings forth error and builds up flesh consciousness. The fruit of this sowing is death and corruption. Every spiritual thought is a seed sown to the Spirit. Spiritual thoughts feed and nourish and build up the spiritual man. The result is life and immortality to the whole man: Spirit, soul, and body.

Spirit—God as the moving force in the universe; Principle as the breath of life in all creation; the principle of life; creative intelligence and life.

We sometimes discover within ourselves a flow of thought that has been evolved independently of the reasoning process and we are puzzled about its origin and its safety as a guide. In its beginnings this seemingly strange source of knowledge is turned aside as a day-dream; again it seems a distant voice, an echo of something that we have heard and forgotten. One should give attention to this unusual and usually faint whispering of Spirit in man. It is the development in man of a greater capacity to know himself and to understand the purpose of creation.

When one concentrates all the faculties on Truth ideas, the conscious mind and superconscious mind blend, and there is a descent of spiritual energies into soul and body. Then the faculties receive new power to express Truth and the body is renewed.

Spirit of truth—The Mind of God in its executive capacity; it carries out the divine plan of the originating

Spirit. It proceeds from the Father and bears witness of the Son.

The Spirit of truth is God's thought projecting into our mind ideas that will build a spiritual consciousness like that of Jesus. The Spirit of truth watches every detail of our life, and when we by affirmation proclaim its presence, it brings new life into our body and prosperity into our affairs.

Spirit of wholeness—The Holy Spirit of the New Testament. In Greek mythology the Holy Spirit is symbolized by the goddess Hygeia. Modern medical men call it the restorative power of nature. (see *Holy Spirit*)

spiritual cosmogony—Spiritual interpretation of the creation of the universe. When science admits that the ether is moved by omnipotent Mind, the Bible will show forth a complete spiritual cosmogony.

spiritual discernment—Intuitive knowing of that which is true of God, or Spirit.

spiritual healer—One who helps man reform so that bodily healing follows as a natural consequence. In order to have bodily perfection it is necessary to bring the mind to a state of righteousness. This is the work of the spiritual healer.

spiritual quickening—Making active according to spiritual standards, by being linked to the activity of God-Mind.

spirituality—The consciousness that relates man directly to his Father-God. It is quickened and grows through prayer and other forms of religious thought and worship.

"spears into pruning-hooks"—(Isa. 2:4). Sharp, penetrating thoughts of cruelty turned into helpful ways.

stand—To hold fearlessly to the truth that Spirit is doing its perfect work and that there is no cause for alarm. Endurance is necessary to a soldier, and everyone who aspires to win the good fight of self must be able to stand against whatever comes. But before we can stand we must be prepared to meet adverse thoughts and overcome unworthy desires.

standards—Man's intellectual standards are determined according to the judgments of the senses. The one true standard of thinking is absolute Truth.

star—Represents man's first awakening before he realizes his Christ wisdom and power. The morning star heralds the coming of light and the glory of the sun. In like progressive unfoldment, the mind has its star of promise, which leads on to wisdom, then to final glory in the sun of righteousness, which is the Son of God.

star of Bethlehem—Symbolizes our inner conviction of our divine sonship. This inner conviction of our ability to accomplish whatever we undertake calls forth the very best in us and helps us to succeed where others of equal ability fail. The accumulated wisdom and experience of a man (the Wise Men from the East) rejoice when faith in one's destiny to do the will of God begins to rise within, and all the riches of wise experience, such as gifts of gold, frankincense, and myrrh, are bestowed on the young child. These gifts represent the subconscious reserve forces of the organism that enter into and form the new man in Christ.

stiff-necked—Self-sufficient, obstinate; descriptive of one who has attained a degree of spiritual dominion but is not obedient to the Spirit of truth.

stillness—A mental state of infinite peace, rest, and tranquillity where man's senses are hushed and he abides in God. "Be still, and know that I am God" (Psalms 46:10).

"still small voice"—The voice of Spirit speaking within the depths one's being. The "still small voice" is not an audible voice. It comes from within as spiritual knowing.

stimulant—Any external element that excites activity not characteristic of man's natural state.

stomach—The stomach stands for the meditative faculty of the mind—its ability to receive ideas, turn them over and over, and get mental nourishment from them.

stone, white (Rev. 2:17)—When we redeem ourselves from bondage to sense, we shall be sustained by the inner or spiritual food ("hidden manna"), which is understanding of Truth and which is the foundation ("a white stone") upon which we build up and develop our true Christ self.

strength—The energy of God. Freedom from weakness; stability of character; power to withstand temptation; capacity to accomplish. Strength is physical, mental, and spiritual. All strength originates in Spirit, the thought and the word spiritually expressed being the manifestation.

stumbling block—Stumbling blocks at first may seem to be in the physical environment, but closer discernment reveals that they are primarily in the mind. Therefore, we should not put additional weight into the already existing obstacles by filling them with the thought-stuff of condemnation. We should not judge others but should strive to overlook their limitations. We should beware how we let our zeal to help others interfere with their freedom of choice.

subconscious mind—The memory mind; memory crystallized into function and form. It is the home of our habits, the storehouse of our past thoughts and experiences. It carries on all the bodily functions such as circulation, breathing, digestion, and so forth. We are not conscious of what goes on in these processes, but divine intelligence works perfectly in all of them unless man interferes through ignorant thinking.

The work of overcoming is carried on largely in the subconscious mind. All past thinking must be redeemed and the whole man, conscious and subconscious, brought into the harmony of the Christ consciousness.

substance—The divine idea of the underlying reality of all things. Substance is everywhere present, pervades all things, and inspires to action. It underlies all manifestation and is the spiritual essence, the living energy out of which everything is made. Through substance all the attributes of Being are expressed. It sustains and enriches any idea that is projected into it.

Divine substance is man's supply. Out of it he forms whatever he will according to his faith and understanding. By entering into the silence, acknowledging divine substance, affirming his faith in and oneness with it, man becomes conscious of substance.

Spiritual realization of divine substance enriches the soil or thought-stuff of the mind. Jesus considered divine substance the treasure field in which He could find the fulfillment of His every need. Every demonstration over mortal limitations is followed by a realization of infinite reality. When man puts away the belief in the reality of matter, there follows a realization of the presence of true substance, of which matter is a mortal concept. Hence this thought-stuff may be made active by holding an affirmation. *The rich substance of the kingdom of God is pouring its plenty perpetually into my mind and affairs, and I am in all ways prospered.*

success—Attainment of a desired goal. Success comes as the result of faithfulness and earnestness in the application of God's law.

When success fails to crown our efforts, we sometimes become discouraged and quit. Then we try to console ourselves with the thought that it is God's will for us to fail. Failure is not God's will, but man lays it to the charge of God to excuse his own feeling of inadequacy and defeat. God's will is health, happiness, and prosperity for every man; and to have all that is good and beautiful is to express God's will for us.

suggestion—A mental process by which one mind influences another mind, or one's subconscious mind is influenced by one's own efforts.

Suggestion and realization differ in that spiritual realization comes from consciously entering into the Truth of Being, while suggestion may be either of Truth or error. The results of suggestion are temporary; spiritual realizations abide.

sun—The realm of consciousness that has been illuminded by Spirit. "The greater light to rule the day" (Gen. 1:16).

superconscious mind—A state of consciousness based on true ideas, on an understanding and realization of spiritual Truth.

"Where there is no vision the people cast off restraint" (Prov. 29:18). Men must see beyond matter and material possessions, or civilization will perish from the earth. If the superconsciousness, or the Christ Mind, is not developed, the people will destroy one another in insane warring for the fleeting things of the world. Preaching the glories of heaven will not reach a mind that has no capacity for the enjoyment of heaven.

The connection between the superconscious mind and the conscious mind is established within—by meditation, by going into the silence, and by speaking the word.

The superconsciousness is man's only sure guide through the maze of the creative process. By trusting to the infallibility of this guide, man opens himself to the inspiration of the Almighty.

supermind—The Christ consciousness; the mind that knows all and is able to accomplish all things because it is one with the Mind of God.

superstitions—Beliefs of those who live on the mere surface of things; beliefs that certain things or occurrences are good or bad omens. Under all conditions and circumstances declare the perfect law of Divine Mind. "Thou shalt be perfect with Jehovah thy God" (Deut. 18:13).

supplication—The earnest prayer or entreaty of the mind for a way of escape from the dominance of sense.

supply—Spiritual substance. Supply often fails to flow

to one whose faith is fixed in some outer source instead of in substance. Jesus understood spiritual substance and could make from it whatever He wished, whenever He wished.

Anxiety about supply can be overcome by a recognition of the omnipresence of Spirit substance and the centering of faith in it as the one source of supply.

supreme Mind—God-Mind. The universal storehouse of all perfect ideas.

supreme voice—The voice of the Spirit of truth within each man.

swaddling clothes—Bands of cloth in which it was customary to wrap newborn babies. They represent confinement to the limitations of the physical nature of this first emanation of divine life, "because there was no room for them in the inn" (outer consciousness).

sword—Represents any weapon that man may turn against his fellow man. The tongue is called a sharp sword. Unloving words pierce like a sword. We reap whatever we sow. As we do to others so is it done to us. If we sow thoughts and words of destruction we will reap them.

sword, flaming—I AM is the gate through which the thinker comes forth from the invisible to the visible, and it is through this gate that he must go to come into the presence of Spirit. "I am the way, and the truth, and the life" (John 14:6). Hence, we take words and go to God. We come into His presence through the I AM gate and we return the same way. On the inner side of the gate is the Garden of Eden, but "the Cherubim, and the flame of a sword" are there, "to keep the way of the tree of life" (Gen. 3:24).

swords into plowshares—Destructive thoughts transformed into instruments of body culture.

symbols—Represent steps in the masonry of the soul. All scriptural symbols have to do with the spiritual progress of man. In the Bible every name stands for an idea and has a meaning that gives a clue to the symbol.

A symbol loses its usefulness when man clings to it as the reality and fails to see the Truth that it represents.

synagogue—Represents an aggregation of religious ideas based on Truth, thoughts that have not yet received the inspiration of the whole Truth. A synagogue also represents a fixed religious state of consciousness.

A Jewish synagogue was a little chapel, where anyone could hear the law read out of the Hebrew Scriptures; or if he was a rabbi he could read out of the law himself. A constant stream of people came and went in the synagogue, and it fitly represents the mind of man, or a phase of man's mind that is given over to religious thought. In the new birth, or regeneration, the rebuilding of man's consciousness begins in this synagogue or religious mentality.

The synagogue of Acts 17:1, 2 in which Paul "for three Sabbath days reasoned with them from the scriptures," is the established religious thought bred in us by tradition, education, and inheritance.

T

tabernacle—Represents the temporal body of man, as the Temple built by Solomon in Jerusalem represents the permanent body. In the wilderness of sense, man worships God in a tent, or a temporary, transitory state of mind, which makes a perishable body. Yet in this flimsy structure are all the furnishings of the great temple that is to be built. So the body of every man is the promise of an imperishable one.

tables of stone—Represent the very foundation of our being, on which are engraved the memories of all our religious experiences.

talents (Matt. 25:14-30)—Symbolize our spiritual

gifts of life, love, truth, substance, intelligence, faith, power, judgment, and will. Every inherent attribute of man's being has its root in God. All the gifts of Spirit are to be used to our fullest capacity.

teacher—Jesus appointed but one teacher in His school: the Spirit of truth, the Comforter in every man. "But the Comforter, *even* the Holy Spirit, whom the Father will send in my name, he shall teach you all things, and bring to you remembrance all that I said unto you" (John 14:25).

telepathy—Thought transference; exchange of thought between persons without visible means of transmission. This is a limited concept of omnipresent knowing. When one becomes spiritually developed he does not send his thought to another, but realizes omnipresent knowing, and the ideas he wishes to communicate are received and understood.

Temple, Solomon's—Metaphysically, a symbol of the regenerated body of man, which when he attains it he will never leave. This enduring temple is built in the understanding of Spirit as the one and only cause of all things.

temptation—A proving, testing, or trying. The temptations in the wilderness (Matt. 4:1-11) represent the desires and ambitions of the untried and untrained forces in the subconsciousness. When in the wilderness, Jesus was tempted by the Adversary, or personality; but with His superior understanding, He withstood the deceptive promises made to Him. When the personality suggested that Jesus make matter out of substance, use His power to rule over others, or do other marvelous things to prove His mastery, He said to the satanic personality, "Get thee hence, Satan."

That the temptations in the wilderness were not physical is quite evident, because there was no mountain from which all the kingdoms of the earth could be seen, nor was there a temple in the wilderness to which the Adversary could have taken Jesus. All these, and many more, including the royal entry of Jesus into Jerusalem riding on an ass, are allegorical representations of the way in which certain states of mind are handled by the initiate.

tents—The flesh bodies of man that he puts on and off again and again. (see *tabernacle*)

thanksgiving—Rendering our grateful thoughts to God for His manifold blessings. "Surely goodness and loving-kindness shall follow me all the days of my life" (Psalms 23:6). We give thanks that this is Truth.

Thanksgiving will keep the heart fresh; for true thanksgiving may be likened to rain falling upon ready soil, refreshing it and increasing its productiveness.

therapy—That phase of metaphysics which treats of divine healing. We are all interested in the soul and how to save it. Those who follow Jesus go one step farther in soul therapy than the average psychoanalyst; they incorporate Spirit with soul and make it the primal source and sustainer of both soul and body. "It is the spirit that giveth life" (John 6:63).

things—Thoughts lowered in vibration to the level of sense perception. The things that appear are the formulations of man's ideas of himself and God. Back of everything is a thought. Still the senses and you will perceive the thought behind the things.

thinking—The formulating process of mind. It is a faculty of the ego, the omnipotent I AM of each one of us. The thinking faculty is the inlet and the outlet of all your ideas. It is active, zealous, impulsive, but not always wise. Its nature is to think, and think it will. If you are ignorant of your office—a prince in the house of David —and stand meekly by and let it think unsifted thoughts, your thinking faculty will prove an unruly servant. Its food is ideas—symbolized in the Gospels as fishes—and it is forever casting its net on the right, on the left, for a draught. You alone can direct where its net shall be cast.

You are the one who says, "Cast the net on the right side" (John 21:6).

The thinking faculty in you makes you a free agent, because it is your creative center; in and through this one power you establish your consciousness—you build your world. Through the volition of this faculty, you can refuse to receive ideas from Christ, you can cut yourself away from the realm of original Truth, or from the illusionary universe in which you are forever unraveling tangled ends and chasing shadows. Thus we see clearly that this faculty is the rock, the foundation upon which the consciousness must be built.

Be no longer a slave to the thinking faculty; command it to be still and know. Stand at the center of your being and say "I and the Father are one" (John 10:30). "I am meek and lowly in heart" (Matt. 11:29). "All authority hath been given unto me in heaven and on earth" (Matt. 28:18). "There is no God else besides me" (Isa. 45:21).

thought—A product of thinking; a mental vibration or impulse. Each thought is an identity that has a central ego, around which all its elements revolve. Thoughts are capable of expressing themselves. Every thought clothes itself in a life form according to the character given it by the thinker. The form is simply the conclusion of the thought.

One of the axiomatic truths of metaphysics is that "thoughts are things." That the mind of man marshals its faculties and literally makes into living entities the thoughts that it entertains is also a foregone conclusion. The word *things* expresses poorly the active and very vital character of the thoughts to which the mind gives life, substance, and intelligence. We see many inanimate "things" around us in the material world. If we compare our creative thoughts with them we get an inferior conception of the marvelous ability of our mind in its creative capacity.

Thought is controlled by the right use of affirmation and denial—by the power of the mind to accept and reject. This power of the mind is the I AM, and it is through the avenue of expression (I AM) that thought control, dominion, and mastery are obtained. Thoughts are controlled by the mind through its power to say "yes" or "no." To "hold a thought" is to affirm or deny a certain proposition both mentally and audibly until the logic of the mind is satisfied and spiritual realization is attained.

thought atmosphere—The surrounding mental climate created by each person in accordance with the character of his thinking. Thoughts of negation build an antagonistic and discordant atmosphere. Thoughts of love and prosperity, of health and faith, create a harmonious mental atmosphere.

thought center—A collection or aggregation of ideas in the mind. Thoughts of one kind are attracted one to another, form in consciousness, group themselves in the body, and build organs through which they manifest. For example, love manifests through the heart.

thought, colony of—Like attracts like. A thought will take up its abode in our consciousness with thoughts of like character. This law of attraction continues until combined thoughts make a colony. This colony of thoughts expresses itself in the cells of the body—for good or ill.

thought power—The moving force within an idea that gives it expression. All structures are built by thought power. This power is transmitted from mind to mind and from mind to body in all living forms.

thought-stuff—The omnipresent, invisible substance ever ready to take form in accordance with one's mental pattern. The thought-stuff of the universe is more sensitive than a phonographic record; it transcribes not only all sounds, but even the slightest vibration of thought.

thought vibrations—Energies sent out by the force and power of thought. All who are in like planes of consciousness with the thinker of the thought receive these thought energies. In this way telepathic messages are sent and received. When one sends thoughts in personal consciousness, the process is laborious and dangerous. There is a law of Spirit that equalizes all forces generated by the mind. This law is in the keeping of divine Principle, and there is neither success nor safety in using thought energies without its guiding wisdom.

time—The limitation of man's consciousness of space. A day is a measure of time in the realm of effects. A sidereal day is that period in which the earth rotates once on its axis. Man divided that period into seconds, minutes, hours, and thus invented time.

Time is the measure that man gives to passing events. The only power in time is what man imparts to it. When man gets into the understanding of the Absolute, he takes his freedom from all bondage of time and declares that time shall no more enter into the substance of his mind or body or affairs.

tithe—A tenth part. In the Old Testament the tithe or tenth is mentioned as a reasonable and just return to the Lord by way of acknowledging Him as the source of supply.

tithing—Giving a tenth of one's supply to God and His work. Tithing is a tacit agreement that man is in partnership with God in the conduct of his finances. This leads to confidence and assurance that whatever is done will bring increase of some kind. "Give, and it shall be given unto you" (Luke 6:38).

Tithing, which is based on a law that cannot fail, establishes method in giving. It brings into the consciousness a sense of divine order that is manifested in one's outer life and affairs as increased efficiency and greater prosperity. It is the surest way ever found to demonstrate plenty, for it is God's own law and way of giving. "Freely ye received, freely give" (Matt. 10:8).

tolerance—Forbearance; allowing to be done without hindering. Tolerance is passive, and good as far as it goes.

Love is active good will. Love takes the initiative in doing and thinking good, and is far superior to tolerance.

tomb of Joseph of Arimathea—A tomb is a resting place; Arimathea represents an aggregation of thoughts of lofty character, a high state of consciousness in man; Joseph represents a state of consciousness in which we are improving spiritually.

The tomb where Jesus was laid to rest represents an elevated, peaceful state of consciousness in which He rested the three days previous to His resurrection. The word of Truth within Jesus did not die, but was quietly spreading from point to point during this period, getting ready for the supreme test: the overcoming of the appearance of death. For us, the tomb represents a high state of consciousness in us in which we improve in character along all lines. We not only grow into a broader understanding but also we increase in vitality and substance. We are resting in God, and at the same time gathering strength for the power of greater demonstrations to follow. In this state of consciousness the word of Truth is not idle, but quietly spreading. This process continues until the whole consciousness is vitalized by the Holy Spirit.

tongues, speaking with—Symbolizes increased ability to express Truth clearly and freely.

traits, inherited—Belief in the authority of our forefathers to determine our physical and mental characteristics. A form of error thinking. "Call no man your father on the earth" (Matt. 23:9).

transcendent God—God above or beyond His universe, apart from it. God is more than His universe; He is prior to and is exalted above it, but at once He is in His universe as the very essence of it. God is both transcendent and immanent.

transfiguration—Supernatural change of appearance that takes place as one experiences the full flow of divine power through his being. A lifting up of the soul that electrifies the body, causing it to shine. An example held before every follower of the Christ, of the glory it is possible to experience through habitual uplift of life and thought.

transgression of the law—Thinking thoughts that violate the principle of mental harmony inherent in Being.

.   **transmutation**—Change in character, from one phase to another. The lifting up of mind and body, from material aspect to spiritual character.

According to modern science this whole universe of forms can be dissolved into energy, from which it may again be formed. Science does not say that the directive and formative power is man, but the Bible so teaches and especially Jesus. Jesus said that all authority was given to Him in heaven and on earth. He manifested His power in a small way by multiplying a few loaves and fishes to feed more than five thousand persons. In various other instances He demonstrated that He had an understanding of the transmutation of substance. He raised His flesh body to an energy level far higher in potential life and substance than any reached before.

transubstantiation—The doctrine that the consecration by the minister of bread and wine changes the material elements to Christ elements, without affecting their appearance. At the Last Supper Jesus taught that the bread and wine which He consecrated were His body and His blood, and He told His followers to partake of them in remembrance of Him. He did not say that these elements were symbols of His blood and body, but that they were essentially the same substance and life as His body. This also has been the teaching of the church, as interpreted by the Council of Trent: "Under each species and under each particle of each species Christ is contained whole and entire."

This doctrine has been attacked both within and without the church, the majority of ministers and laymen accepting it on faith as in some way related to the miraculous. But the discoveries of the elemental character of matter by modern science are revealing the universal unity of substance and the possibility of its transformation from one thing to another by changing the number of arrangement of the electrons in the atom.

treatment—Spiritual realization of God's Truth for oneself or another. Spiritual process, or prayer, by which man receives the healing power of God.

A treatment is a prayer of faith and understanding for healing, harmony, wisdom, prosperity, or any other good that man may desire. Its object is to raise the consciousness of the one being treated to a high spiritual consciousness through which healing is accomplished.

trees—Represent nerves, and nerves are expressions of thoughts of unity. They connect thought centers. The trees growing on both sides of the river represent the nerves radiating from the vital flow on each side of the spinal column, and connecting and unifying the whole organism.

From the center of our being there spreads into every department of mind and body, the life-giving, everbearing tree of the Spirit of God. Its fruits are intelligence to the mind, substance to the body, and life to the entire being.

tree, oak—An oak tree in itself stands for something very strong and protective; but in Hebrew it has a deeper significance than this. The word comes from the root from which is derived the word *Elohim;* so we are reminded of the truth that those who trust God as their defense, as their refuge, their fortress, and dwell "in the secret place of the Most High, shall abide under the shadow of the Almighty," and shall not only be kept from all evil and its results, but shall continue to grow and unfold in understanding, in spirituality, and in every good.

"tree of life" (Gen. 2:9).—The eternal, omnipresent life of God that is within man. The tree of life "in the midst of the garden" is the innate, indwelling idea of immortal life, and the fruit of that tree is the consciousness of eternal life in the body.

The "tree of life" (figuratively in the midst of the garden) manifests in the body as a reserve force. The brain is the center, the solar plexus is the subcenter, and there are innumerable minor centers throughout the organism, the spinal cord, and nervous system. A conservation of the life and substance of the organism is necessary to its spiritualization and redemption.

"tree of the knowledge of good and evil" (Gen. 2:9)—Indicates a dual state of consciousness, a belief in both good and error, which eventually drives man out of the garden (his body temple).

tree, olive—Growing both under and above water, represents the restoration of unity between the material and spiritual, or God and man.

trinity—The religious terms for the trinity are Father, Son, and Holy Spirit. The metaphysical terms are mind, idea, and expression.

Father is the source, origin, essence, root, creator of all. *Son* is that which proceeds from, is begotten of the Father, like Him in nature, and essentially all that the Father is. *Holy Spirit* is God's word in movement: the working, moving, breathing, brooding of Spirit, made known to men through revelation, inspiration, and guidance. The Holy Spirit is the Comforter who will bring all things to their remembrance.

The doctrine of the trinity is often a stumbling block, because we find it difficult to understand how three persons can be one. Three persons cannot be one, and theology will always be a mystery until theologians become metaphysicians.

God is the name of the all-encompassing Mind. Christ is the name of the all-loving Mind. Holy Spirit is the all-active manifestation. These three are one fundamental Mind in its three creative aspects.

trouble—Calamity, difficulty, disaster; the sure result of wrong thinking. All economic, social, and personal trouble can be traced back to selfishness of the sense man. When spiritual man takes control of mind substance, all trouble of every kind dissolves into thin air.

trumpets and cymbals (Ezra 3:10)—The trumpets and cymbals in the hands of the priests and Levites are the thrills and waves of harmonious energy. They go to every part of our mind and our body when we rejoice in Spirit, when our heart is filled with gratitude, and we express ourselves in thanksgiving to the Author of our being.

Truth—The Absolute; that which accords with God as divine principle; that which is, has been, and ever will be; that which eternally is. The Truth of God is reality: "the same yesterday and to-day, *yea* and for ever." The verities of being are eternal and have always existed. Truth abides in fullness at the very core of man's being. As his consciousness (awareness) expands, he touches the everlasting Truth. What seems new is but the unveiling of that which always has been.

The basic principle of Truth is that the mind of each individual may be consciously unified with Divine Mind through the indwelling Christ. By affirming at-one-ment with God-Mind, we eventually realize that perfect mind which was in Christ Jesus.

Truth, road of—The straight and narrow path along which Spirit directs, and which proves so smooth and safe that one refuses to allow oneself to be misled by habit into trusting sense perception.

Truth, source of—God is a special, personal Father to all His children, and from no other source can they get absolute Truth.

truth, Spirit of—God's thought projecting into our mind ideas that will build spiritual consciousness like that of Jesus. The Spirit of truth watches every detail of our life. When we ask and by affirmation proclaim its presence, it brings new life into both mind and body and moves us to observe spiritual and physical laws that restore health.

twelve—Metaphysically, twelve always refers to spiritual fulfillment. "And Elijah took twelve stones, according to the number of the tribes of the sons of Jacob . . . And with the stones he built an altar in the name of Jehovah" (I Kings 18:31, 32). The twelve stones represent the twelve most important nerve centers in the body. All material things represent spiritual realities.

Before we can realize unfettered power we must establish permanent resolutions of purity and covenants of conformity with the higher law of obedience. Elijah repaired the altar of Jehovah that had been thrown down. Obedience seems a simple matter, but the twelve fundamental faculties enter into its perfect expression. Elijah took twelve stones and fitted them together to form the altar, each stone representing one of the sons of Jacob, who won the name *Israel* in recognition of his perseverance toward perfection.

U

understanding—God is supreme knowing. That in man which comprehends is understanding; it knows and comprehends in wisdom. Its comparisons are not made in the realm of form, but in the realm of ideas. It knows how to accomplish things. Spiritual discernment reveals that knowledge and intelligence are auxiliary to understanding.

There are two ways of getting understanding. One is by following the guidance of Spirit that dwells within, and the other is to go blindly ahead and learn by hard experience.

Intellectual understanding of Truth is a tremendous step in advance of sense consciousness, and its possession brings a temptation to use for selfish ends the wisdom and power thereby revealed.

Spiritual understanding is the quickening of the Spirit within. Spiritual understanding is the ability of the mind to apprehend and realize the laws of thought and the relation of ideas one to another.

unfoldment—Bringing out by successive development; growth. As we unfold spiritually day by day, Spirit reveals more and more good to us. (see *I Cor. 2:9*)

union with God—Unification of our consciousness with that of God-Mind. This is the Christ consciousness. "I and the Father are one" (John 10:30).

unity—Universal oneness of God, man, and all creation. The only real unity is in Spirit. It is found nowhere else because personality always strives for its own success and aims for the good of the personal man, instead of the good of all men.

Man makes conscious unity with God first at the center of spirituality, this center having its basis of action in the top of the head. The only way to establish unity with the Father-Mind is by prayer. God's name is I AM. Our name is I AM. Speaking this name in the silence, recognizing that it is God's name and ours, we establish conscious unity with Him.

universal—All-encompassing. There is one life force: the creative universal life, even God. This life is eternal and infinite, from everlasting to everlasting.

universal resource—Omnipresent cosmic substance and reality from which all supply flows to man by means of his spoken word.

universal Spirit—Omnipresent, omnipotent, and omniscient God.

universal substance—The omnipresent mind stuff that can be molded to man's use through his thinking; mind substance.

universal urge—The urge toward perfection. In man this urge is the spiritual seed of the Christ, which ever seeks to unfold its divine nature.

universe—The total of all that is. It was first expressed as an idea in Divine Mind and later made manifest; that is, it became visible to the five senses by means of the creative power, the Word.

unreal—That which is temporal or transient; not based on Truth. Evil is the perfect example of the unreal. As soon as divine law is applied, the unreal, evil, has no existence. In Truth, it is nothing.

upper chamber—A higher state of consciousness attained through prayer or by going into the silence. "And when they were come in, they went up into the upper chamber, where they were abiding" (Acts 1:13).

The "upper chamber" to which the apostles went for the baptism of the Holy Spirit is the high state of mind that we assume in thinking about spiritual things. It may be attained through prayer, going into the silence with true words, or in meditation.

V

vegetarian—One who abstains from eating animal food or products. "And God said, Behold, I have given you every herb yielding seed, which is upon the face of all the earth, and every tree, in which is the fruit of a tree yielding seed; to you it shall be for food" (Gen. 1:29)

Vegetarianism is one of the ways to real health, because it requires, in a measure, the keeping of the spiritual law

veil of the Temple—That in the body which has shut out the light of Spirit and has hindered man from consciously standing in the presence of God. The rending of the veil of the Temple pictures a letting go of the belief in the reality of material consciousness. The relinquishment of the soul to God is the final giving up of all human ambitions and aims.

verities, eternal—The truths of Being, which are without beginning and without end; facts of existence.

vessels, holy—(I Kings 8:4). The thoughts that lie back of and form the various organs of the body. The vessels that had been taken from the Temple by Nebuchadnezzar and returned by Cyrus (Ezra 16:8) represent our capacity to comprehend and our ability to measure and appreciate life, love, and Truth.

vessels of silver—Fruit of one's experience in the sense consciousness added to one's innate spiritual consciousness.

vesture of Jesus—(John 19:23). Symbolizes the consciousness of unity, which is the inner conviction of all things. (see *coat without seam*)

vibrations—The rate at which all forces move. One of the greatest discoveries of all ages is that of physical science which shows that all things have their source and being in vibrations. What Jesus taught so profoundly in symbols about the riches of the kingdom of the heavens has now been proved true.

The whole universe is in vibration, and that vibration is under law. Chaos would result if the law were not supreme. Each particular thing has its rate of vibration. Heat, light, and color are different rates of vibration in one field of primal energy. Different colors are caused by the different frequencies of the vibrations as they strike the eye. But what causes vibration? We answer, mind.

vibrations, thought—Energies sent out by the force and power of thought.

vine and branches—The I AM within us is the vine, our faculties are the branches, and the perfect body is the fruit. The life current as it comes from the universal source is combined in vine, branches, and fruit, and it is on this free-flowing inner force that we fix our attention when we demonstrate the power of Spirit. Material symbols are likely to be misleading unless we remember always to get the spiritual import of their I AM application.

vineyard—The fruit of the vine is a symbol of life. Jesus said, "I am the vine." The vineyard represents manifest man, or humanity which was planted in perfection, and perfection is its destiny.

virgins—The ten virgins represent the senses. The senses are five, in number but have a twofold action—five in the inner realm and five in the outer world. The way to supply oil for the lamps of the virgins, even of the foolish ones is to affirm that the life source, Spirit, from which comes the power of hearing, smelling, seeing, feeling, and tasting, is not material but spiritual. Each sense has an inner counterpart, which is connected with the one life, from which it draws its oil, or life current. There is a soul eye and a soul ear, and these on their inner side are in direct contact with Spirit. But their outer side is in touch with the intellect and through the intellect with the formed organ of sense in the body. It is on this intellectual plane that mortal mind has its citadel and causes so much trouble with the outer organs.

vision, spiritual—Seeing God as the foundation of all, the sources of all, and the substance of all. Seeing the good, the true, and the beautiful everywhere. In this manner is the eye single and vision perfected.

voice—"Faculty or power of utterance" (Webster). The power center in the throat controls all the vibratory energies of this organism. It is the open door between the formless and the formed worlds of vibrations pertaining to the expression of sound. Every word that goes forth receives its specific character from the power faculty. Therefore, the voice is the most direct avenue of expression of consciousness.

Spirit is the "still small voice" in every man that hears and blesses and uplifts. Spirit is made manifest as perfect wholeness through the illumined mind.

The art of listening to the inner voice and obeying it is well-worth developing. Then it is that the Christ of one's life calls out, "Put out into the deep, and let down your nets for a draught." When the thinking faculty is obedient and does as it is told, it is always rewarded with a multitude of new ideas (fishes).

W

wait on the Lord—When we listen to the voice of Spirit we are waiting on the Lord.

walk by the Spirit—Means to acknowledge the power of the Christ Spirit within mind and body as the dominating force.

watch, high—Persistent looking toward the fulfillment of divine ideals.

watchman—A spiritually developed person who sees within and without, and with the word of command challenges anything negative.

water—In its different aspects water represents weakness and negativeness, cleansing, mental potentiality, and in some cases life, or vital energy.

In one of its aspects, water represents negativeness. The individual who allows himself to become negative to the good finds himself uncertain and unstable in his mind, and often becomes so submerged in the waters of negation that his physical condition is low. Weak sympathy with error and the results of error helps to produce this condition. To be positive toward the good it is very necessary that one have right ideas of God, that one know Him as all good.

Water also represents the great mass of thoughts that conform to environment. Every thought leaves its form in the consciousness, and all the weak characterless words and expressions gather in the subconscious mind as water gathers in holes. When we get discouraged or disappointed and "give up," the undertow of life sweeps this flood of negative thought over us, and we are conscious of bodily weakness of some sort. When we know the Truth, and "brace up," however, the waters are confined to their natural channels again and our strength is restored.

From the intellectual viewpoint water represents cleansing. When John the Baptist baptized with water, he washed away the sins of an external character. His baptism did not enter into the subconsciousness. It takes something more powerful than water to purify the error conditions accumulated by the soul in its many incarnations. The presence of God through Christ is necessary to purify this part of man.

water, above and below the firmament—In every mental proposition we have an above and a below. Above the firmament are the unexpressed capacities (waters) of the conscious mind resting in faith in Divine Mind. In this realm when "God says," the word is instantly fulfilled; the mental image of the word is registered in consciousness.

Below the firmament are the expressed capacities (waters) of the subconscious mind, which may be called memory but has not power to do original thinking. To reach the subconscious realm, the word must be declared consciously, and then from this firm starting point, directed down into the subconscious realm, where the redemptive work is carried on.

water, walk on—Water (the sea) represents mental potentiality. The race thoughts have formed a sea of thought, and to walk over it safely requires that one have faith in oneself. Faith necessary to accomplish so great an undertaking comes from understanding—understanding of God and man and the law of mastery given to man. If one is to walk on the waves of troubled thought without sinking, he must become established in the faith of Spirit through Christ.

waterpots—The "six waterpots of stone" (John 2:6, 7) represent the six nerve centers in the body, which are filled with the water of life, nerve fluid.

The waterpots filled to the brim with water by the servants show the extent to which God is prepared to fulfill the transformation from natural life to spiritual life through the power of the word.

This transformation into vitalizing Spirit is accomplished by adding to every word a spiritual idea. The idea of omnipresent life will then quicken the natural life in man, and it will make conscious contact with the one life and draw it out for the benefit of the many.

way, the—The I AM in man, the open door to the kingdom of God. (see *Christ* and *Jesus*)

wealth—True wealth is a state of consciousness, the consciousness of God as man's supply. Spiritual wealth expresses itself as faith, love, wisdom, substance, joy, and so on. Material wealth expresses as worldly riches, possessions of an earthly nature.

wedding garment—Garments represent the outer clothing of the mind. The "wedding garment" (Matt. 22:11) is the role of righteousness (right-use-ness) and is symbolical of a state of consciousness in which there is special preparation for the union unique. In other words, our external thinking must be in harmony with the inner revelation before we can make complete union with the Christ.

well—Symbolizes inspiration through the intellect alone. The well of living water (John 4:10-14) in man is the fount of inspiration within his consciousness, which flows forth peacefully, majestically, vitalizing and renewing mind and body.

well-beloved—The Christ, the ideal man.

wholeness—The perfect unification and expression of man as Spirit, soul, and body. True healing means to make whole. It is brought about by regeneration.

widow—One who has lost sight of God as support. When the conscious mind has ceased to be positive, the subconscious mind becomes like a "widow." The conscious unity between the mind and the vitality of the organism has been severed, and there is lack and burden (debt). This takes place eventually in all who do not consciously take possession of the twelve faculties in the organism.

The "widow" in Luke 18:1-5 typifies a belief in lack. Lack is not good in itself, but it serves to call man's attention to the law (judge). Dependence on the judgments of the law, without consciousness of love, subjects one to hard experience and laborious expression.

Jesus portrays the power of affirmative prayer, or repeated silent demands for justice, as a widow, one bereft of worldly protection and power. Under her persistence even the ungodly judge succumbs. The unceasing prayer of faith is commanded in the Scriptures, in various places.

widow of Zarephath—The widow of Zarephath, to whom Elijah was sent for sustenance, represents love bereft of wisdom. She represents the divine feminine, while Elijah here is the divine masculine or wisdom. Separated they are both in a state of semi-starvation but when they are joined in consciousness, increase at once begins and lack ceases. "The jar of meal wasted not, neither did the cruse of oil fail" (I King 17:9-16).

wife, taking a—Represents a unification of the I AM with the affections.

wilderness—In individual consciousness the wilderness is symbolical of the multitude of undisciplined and uncultivated thoughts.

will, the—The will is the executive faculty of the mind, the determining factor in man. What man wills or decrees comes to pass in his experience. "Thou shalt also decree a thing, and it shall be established unto thee" (Job 22:28).

The will is the center in mind and body around which

revolve all the activities that constitute consciousness. It is the avenue through which the I AM expresses its potentiality.

The will may be said to be the man, because it is the directive power that determines character formation. When man wills to do the will of God, he exercises his individual will in wisdom, love, and spiritual understanding; he builds spiritual character.

The use of the will is very important in making demonstrations. One must be very persistent since persistence is essential to demonstration. Truth builds the perfect body, and the will must resolutely lay hold and keep hold of the word of Truth until the word becomes flesh.

will and desire—Desire is a reaching out of the mind for satisfaction. Will is the controlling, directing faculty of mind. One may have the desire to be well and yet not have the will to be well.

will and I AM—The will is the executive faculty of the mind and carries out the edicts of the I AM. All thoughts that go in and out of man's consciousness pass the gate at which sits the will. If the will understands its office, the character and value of every thought are inquired into and a certain tribute is exacted for the benefit of the whole man.

will and wisdom—When the will of man adheres to wisdom faithfully and carries out in its work the plans that are idealized in wisdom, it creates in man a consciousness of harmony and peace. Spirit breathes into such an individual continually the inspiration and knowledge necessary to give him superior understanding.

will, divine—(see *God, will of*)

will, personal—The adversary in sense-conscious will. He usurps power and considers himself the rightful ruler. This erroneous belief relating to personal will is discerned and adjusted by spiritual thoughts attained through prayer.

This adversary troubles us because we strive to maintain personal freedom instead of submitting to divine guidance. Self-confidence is a virtue when founded on the Truth of Being, but when it arises from the personal consciousness it keeps man from his dominion.

wind, east—Life currents that come from within and surround the whole being; the executive power of mind clearing the way to higher states of consciousness.

wine—Symbolizes the vitality that forms the connecting link between soul and body. It represents an all-pervading, free essence that is generated from the nerve substance, or water of life. The wine of life, or vitality of the organism, must be available in large quantities before a blending of thoughts, or of soul and body (wedding), can be made successfully. When the new Christ life comes into a mind where old beliefs concerning the body have been held, the body is transformed into its innate spiritual perfection.

wings—Symbolize freedom from material limitations.

wisdom—Intuitive knowing; spiritual intuition; the voice of God within as the source of our understanding; mental action based on the Christ Truth within. Wisdom includes judgment, discrimination, intuition, and all the departments of mind that come under the head of knowing. This "knowing" capacity transcends intellectual knowledge. Spiritual discernment always places wisdom above the other faculties of the mind and reveals that knowledge and intelligence are auxiliary to understanding.

wisdom and divine understanding—These attributes come from the Spirit of Christ within us. The price that we must pay for the conscious attainment of divine wisdom and understanding is the letting go of the personal self with its limited beliefs. Paul saw the Christ waiting at the door of every soul when he wrote: "Awake, thou that sleepest, and arise from the dead, and Christ shall shine upon thee" (Eph. 5:17).

wisdom, worldly—Wisdom is the ability to use knowledge. Worldly wisdom is knowledge of worldly things, with the ability to use them.

Wise Men—The Wise Men of the East who came to visit the baby Jesus may be likened to the stored-up resources of the soul that rise to the surface when its depths are stirred by a great spiritual revelation. In scriptural symbology *East* always means the within.

The gold, frankincense, and myrrh that the Wise Men brought when Jesus was born are symbolical of the inner resources open to the Christ child. They may be the stored-up deeds and thoughts of previous incarnations that wisdom within (the Wise Men) carefully guards and gives to the soul as an inheritance. Thus no good thought or deed is ever lost in the divine economy.

wishing—A wish is a superficial expression of desire, and is only fleeting. The patience, perseverance, and intense eagerness necessary to spiritual growth cannot come from anything as shallow as a wish.

Wishing will give way to desire when one consecrates himself wholly to God and follows up his consecration with prayer and meditation on Truth.

wolves—Devouring thoughts. They represent fear thoughts, thoughts of lack, and all thoughts that rob one of life and substance ideas.

woman—The feminine phase of man. In Genesis 2:18-25 woman typifies love in the soul not yet developed and established in substance.

woman, Greek—Signifies the intuitive perception of Truth reflected into the intellect from the soul. She also represents the unspiritualized love that is natural to the body.

Word—The agency by which God reveals Himself in some measure to all men, but to greater degree to highly developed souls; the thought of God or the sum total of God's creative power. The Word gives order and regularity to the movement of things and is the divine dynamic, the energy and self-revelation of God.

The Word of God is immanent in man and all the universe. All original creation is carried forward by and through man's conscious recognition of this mighty One.

Man is the consummation of the Word. His spirit has within it the concentration of all that is contained within the Word. God being perfect, His idea, thought, Word, must be perfect. Jesus expresses this perfect Word of God as spiritual man. "The Word became flesh, and dwelt among us" (John 1:14).

Word, creative—The creative idea in Divine Mind, which may be expressed by man when he has fulfilled the law of expression. All words are formative, but not all words are creative. The creative Word lays hold of Spirit substance and power. When Jesus said with a loud voice to Lazarus, "Come forth," (John 11:43) He had contact with the creative Word. As spirituality increases we fulfill the law. Our word has power and is creative.

word, healing—As man is quickened with spiritual faith his word is endowed with power. It becomes so charged with spiritual energy he is enabled to heal all manner of diseases, even at a distance. "The supplication [word] of a righteous man availeth much" (James 5:16).

word, reproving—A word of authoritative command; a form of vigorous denial that reaches the error belief behind the disease. "And Jesus rebuked him, saying, Hold thy peace, and come out of him" (Mark 1:25).

words—The vehicles through which ideas make themselves manifest. Words that have in them the realization of perfect, everywhere-present, always-present divine life, and our oneness with this life, are dominant in the restoration of life and health.

When spiritual words abide in man's consciousness, the word or thought formed in intellectual and sense mind must give way to the higher principles of Being. The whole consciousness is then raised to a more spiritual plane. Affirmations of words or of Truth realized in consciousness bring the mind into just the right attitude to receive light, and power, and guidance from Spirit.

work, object of—The true object of all work is to express the powers of one's being and to benefit mankind.

work in consciousness—To erase persistent forms of manifest negations through the increased use of denials and affirmations is often necessary. Man does the works that Jesus did by entering into the same consciousness that He was in—the realization of oneness with the Father.

world, the—A state of consciousness formed through the belief in the reality of things external. It leads one to follow standards of living based on man's opinions rather than on Truth. The world is overcome by our denying that it has any power over us and affirming freedom in Christ.

world, end of—"The end of the age," as Ferrar Fenton puts it, is the point in consciousness where true thoughts are in the majority, and error thoughts have lost their hold. This is the final consummation of the regenerative process. Everything that has been stored in consciousness is brought forth and becomes of visible, practical value to man.

. The end of the world prophesied in the Bible will come as a thief in the night—quietly, silently. Those who are wrapped up in the things of sense will suddenly awake to the consciousness that they have lost their all, that this too solid earth has dissolved and left them without a place of action for their material thoughts.

worship—When one worships he bestows his love on, or identifies himself with, the things of Spirit. Worship represents the efforts of man to sustain a right mental attitude toward God.

wrath of God—Some Bible authorities claim that the "wrath of God" (Rom. 1:18) might with equal propriety be translated the "blessing of God." We know that after the destruction of limited and inferior thoughts and forms of life, other and higher thoughts and forms take their place, and the change is actually a blessing in the end. So even the "wrath" that comes to our fleshly tabernacles, when we persist in holding them in material thought, is ultimately a blessing. When we are loving and nonresistant we do not suffer under the transformations that go on when the Mosaic law is being carried out. The "wrath of God" is really the working out of the law of Being for the individual who does not conform to the law but thinks and acts in opposition to it.

Y

Yahweh—The original Hebrew form of *Jehovah*. It means "the self-existent one" who reveals Himself to His creation and through His creation.

Yahweh revealed Himself to Jesus as the Father within; Yahweh revealed himself to Moses as "I AM THAT I AM" (Exod. 3:14).

years—The measure of passing events. They constitute what we call time. But man's bodily condition depends on his state of mind. No two persons the same age are in exactly the same bodily condition. This shows that years do not make man young or old. "For as he thinketh within himself, so is he" (Prov. 23:7).

youth—The natural estate of all men. The buoyancy and joy of youth should be cultivated enthusiastically as the years advance. Deep in the subconscious mind is the God idea of eternal youth. It may have become dormant and needs to be awakened. Deny the belief in feebleness as the foolish fallacy of the race mind. Affirm and express the wondrous dynamic life of God and you will remain forever young.

Z

zeal—Intensity, ardor, enthusiasm; the inward fire of the soul that urges man onward, regardless of the intellectual mind of caution and conservatism.

Zeal is the mighty force that incites the winds, the tides, the storms; it urges the planet on its course, and spurs the ant to greater exertion. It is the urge behind all things. Zeal is the affirmative impulse of existence, its command is "Go forward!"

"The zeal of thy house hath eaten me up" (Psalms 69:9) means that the zeal faculty has become so active intellectually that it has consumed the vitality and left nothing for spiritual growth. One may become so zealous for the spread of Truth as to bring on nervous prostration. "Take time to be holy." Turn a portion of your zeal to do God's will; to the establishing of His kingdom within you. Do not put all your enthusiasm into teaching, preaching, healing, and helping others; help your own soul. Do not let your zeal run away with your judgment. When zeal and judgment work together great things can be accomplished.

zone, spiritual—Through His spiritual attainments Jesus formed a spiritual zone in the earth's mental atmosphere. His followers make connection with that zone when they pray in His "name." He stated this fact in John 14:2, "I go to prepare a place for you." Simon Peter said, "Lord, whither goest thou?" Jesus answered him, "Whither I go, thou canst not follow me now; but thou shall follow afterwards" (John 13:36).

Additional books by Charles Fillmore and their original publication dates

Christian Healing—1909
Talks on Truth—1926
The Twelve Powers of Man—1930
Metaphysical Bible Dictionary—1931
Mysteries of Genesis—1936
Prosperity—1936
Jesus Christ Heals—1939
Teach Us to Pray—1941
    (Coauthored with Cora Dedrick Fillmore)
Mysteries of John—1946
Atom-Smashing Power of Mind—1949
Keep a True Lent—1953
The Revealing Word—1959
Dynamics for Living—1967
    (Selected and arranged by Warren Meyer)
The Charles Fillmore Concordance—1975
    (Compiled by Clinton E. Bernard)

Books by Myrtle Fillmore

Wee Wisdom's Way—1894
    (No longer available)
Myrtle Fillmore's Healing Letters—1954
    (Edited by Francis W. Foulkes—originally published
    as *The Letters of Myrtle Fillmore*)
How to Let God Help You—1956

Book by Cora Dedrick Fillmore

Christ Enthroned in Man—1937

Date shown is year originally published.